Snuff, Snus and Chew

a recipe book

edited by

Robert C.A. Goff

Dreamsplice
Christiansburg, Virginia

Snuff, Snus and Chew: a recipe book

Dreamsplice
3462 Dairy Road
Christiansburg, VA 24073

www.dreamsplice.com

Cover design by Robert C.A. Goff, Copyright © 2023 by Dreamsplice

ISBN 13: 979-8-9867728-2-0

Library of Congress Control Number: 2023907594

First Edition: June 2023

Front cover image by forum member @jojjas.

Other Works by Robert C.A. Goff

Fantasy-fiction by Robert C.A. Goff
Ternaria: Legacy of a Careless Age

Science-fiction by Robert C.A. Goff
Impact Mitigation and other Science-fiction Short Stories

Non-fiction by Robert C.A. Goff
In the Ozone: collected essays, poems and non-fiction
Climbing Out: Grand Canyon Hikes 1997-2006
Just Walking Home: AT Hikes 1996-2013
How to Read a US Roadmap
Grow Your Own Cigars: growing, curing and finishing tobacco at home
Blend Your Own Pipe Tobacco: 52 recipes with 52 color labels
Ninety More Pipe Blends: 90 more recipes with 90 color labels
The Cigar Artistry of Marc Langanes: torcedor and photographer
Tobacco Plant Varieties for Home Growers
It Could Have Gone Either Way: the times I almost died

Fantasy-fiction by Robert C.A. Goff and Micah M.A. Goff

The Counterspell Chronicle
Counterspell: Guardian of the Ruins
Counterspell: The Second Law
Counterspell: Age of Fools [upcoming]

Acknowledgments

Thank you to all the members of the Fair Trade Tobacco Forum who have created the recipes and commentary included in this book. This collection presented a unique opportunity for me to include the forum user name for each of the contributors. You will find them in both the table of contents as well as the individual recipes and comments. Consider this, collectively, *your book*. And forgive me if, in my editing zeal, I have watered down your personal writing styles.

Bob

Dedication

To my son, Micah.

page 5

Contents

Chew

Nasal Snuff

Other Preparations

Appendix: Ingredient Lists

Introduction

As with all of my books on the subject of tobacco, all of this content is available already on the Fair Trade Tobacco forum (FTT) at https://fairtradetobacco.com, scattered among its more than 200,000 posts that have accumulated since the forum's birth in 2011. Don Carey, of Whole Leaf Tobacco (https://wholeleaftobacco.com) founded the forum, and its thousands of members have created its invaluable content. In this book, I have sifted through the morass of posts in the "Smokeless" forum of FTT, and assembled the most useful content in a more or less readable form.

I have to confess, right from the start, that I have never used smokeless tobacco, and have never tested any of the recipes that I present here. The recipes are the forum members' own. Where there is any commentary by other members, I have included that, but only if it is directly relevant to the stated recipe.

To compile this collection, I have carefully read through over 260 "Smokeless" threads, comprised of thousands of individual posts. Some of them wander off-topic, or consist of common questions with answers that are covered in other threads. I have selected meaningful recipes along with helpful advice and guidance. The seemingly simple task of sorting out whether or not a recipe was for dry nasal snuff, ground oral snus or shredded chew was sometimes a challenge.

CAUTION: Many of the recipes included in this volume advise the use of strong alkali (caustic) solutions. These have the potential to not only cause chemical burns to your skin, but become a medical emergency if you get some in your eyes. Strong alkali solutions can cause permanent eye damage within just a few minutes. Handle these solutions with great care. If some of it splashes into your eye, immediately rinse your eye with running water for 10 minutes. You should not wait for medical care prior to rinsing the affected eye. After rinsing, *always* seek immediate medical attention. Your eyesight may be at risk. Consider wearing safety goggles during alkali prep.

The History of Snuff, Snus and Chew (confusion and clarity)
by squeezyjohn

The confusion is an historical one connected with the spread around the globe of different tobacco types, which took them through several languages as well!
WARNING: LONG ETYMOLOGICAL ESSAY FOLLOWS

Snuff is an old English term for anything powdered you took medicinally through the nostrils, related to the word sniff. It was one of the many techniques used to get old herbal remedies into the body, and we still use related words like snuffling or snuffly to describe the sound of a person with a cold (or an animal that sounds similar).

Around the year 1500 the first travelers to the new world of the Americas discovered tobacco being used by the native elders in a snuff format, via types of tubes, and brought the plant back with them to Spain and Portugal, where it was touted as a new medicine to be used as a powdered form taken in to the nostrils.

In the 1560s a Frenchman called Jean Nicot was ambassador in Lisbon. He sent some tobacco back to Paris, where Queen Catherine had been suffering from chronic headaches, and advised her to use it to relieve the pain. It worked very well, and became fashionable amongst upper class and courtly circles throughout France and wider Europe. Jean Nicot's name lives in history as the Latin name of the plant family

Nicotiana...and by association, the chemical nicotine is also named after him.

Snuff gained it's English name when it arrived in the English courts of the early 1600s, as this was already the name for a medicine taken nasally. Over time, the word snuff became almost exclusively associated with this form of tobacco. Meanwhile, this nasal tobacco spread to Sweden via the courts as well. The word Snus is of a similar Germanic origin to the English word snuff, and is first documented in Swedish in 1637. At that time it still referred to nasal snuff. By the 1700s, nasal "snus" was very popular in Sweden, and tobacco farming had become a common thing throughout the country (unlike in England, which relied on it's American colonies to provide tobacco).

By the early 1800s, tobacco use had filtered down to all levels of Swedish Society, however the farmers and workers had taken to using their ground up tobacco by wetting it a little, and placing it in their upper lips, instead of using their noses. Presumably this was an easier way to use the product while actively working. This method became the default way of using snus, while nasal snuff was rapidly going out of fashion amongst the upper classes. Certain brands and recipes were set up in this period, including Ljunglof's Ettan (Ettan means number one in Swedish) which is still available today, made by Swedish Match. Many other brands followed including Generalsnus (regular snus) and Röda Lacket (Red Seal).

In the late 1800s, more than a million Swedes crossed the Atlantic to set up new lives in the USA, and brought their snus habit with them. Brands were set up to serve the demand, and some used old Swedish names like Copenhagen and Red Seal. Throughout the 1900s the styles of recipe used in this oral tobacco diverged in it's Swedish homeland and in the USA, so the products now are very distinct from each other. The word snus was still in common use as an alternative to dip as late as the 1950s in some parts of the USA. Nowadays, "dip" or "snuff" is the normal word used in the states to describe American moist oral tobacco [even though dry, nasal snuff is still its own distinct product in the US].

But the term dip has yet another nasal-snuff related origin from much earlier in history. During the British colonial period, the French-inspired upper-class snuff habit had also made the journey across the Atlantic. Whereas cigars became the favourite form of tobacco use amongst gentlemen, ladies took to dipping a moistened stick in nasal snuff and rubbing it in to their gums, which was considered more discrete and ladylike than either snorting it or smoking cigars! Dipping became the term for this, and at some point in the 1900s the term became confused with the recently imported Swedish form of using snus in the upper lip. The American preference for dipping in the lower lip also happened at some point in time near this.

So there you have it. Snuff, snus, dip. It's all really the same thing, separated by cultural evolution over time, and several language changes.

Basic Guidelines

Dry Nasal Snuff:
In its most elementary form, this is simply pure tobacco leaf lamina ground into a fine powder. It can be made from any variety of tobacco.

Most recipes for dry nasal snuff are more elaborate, involving cooking, the addition of alkali (to increase nicotine availability), table salt, flavorants (essential oils, extracts, alcoholic beverages or fruit juices), and sometimes humectants.

Oral Snus:
As with nasal snuff, any variety of tobacco can be used or blended, depending on personal preferences. Leaf stems, which contain a lower nicotine concentration than the lamina, are often ground, and added to the ground leaf lamina, for both bulk and texture. The mixture is usually cooked in some manner (often for hours or days), and usually has alkali added after the initial cooking, to increase the nicotine availability.

The assortment of salt, herbs, spices, juices and flavorants is an open-ended choice. Addition of humectants (such as propylene glycol and glycerin) is common, since the final product is intended to be stored, perhaps long-term, in a fairly moist state.

Chew:
Any tobacco variety can be used for chew, depending on your personal preference.

Chew can be simply a piece of leaf moist enough to not initially crumble. The leaf can be unaltered, twisted, braided, etc. Many recipes call for cooking, flavorings, and sometimes alkali. It can be coarsely chopped, shredded or blended with multiple varieties.

Cooking Methods:
Smokeless preparations can be baked in an oven, in an open pan. They can be slow-cooked in an open pot. Cooking times vary by tradition and preference. Multiple, differing recipes can be cooked within sealed canning jars (Mason jars) simultaneously, without their flavors mingling. Jars are usually heated within a water bath or pressure cooker. To prevent the jars from floating and tipping over during cooking, they should be held in place or weighted. Increasing pressure within a tipped-over canning jar will force out liquid, rather than water vapor.

Commercial Smokeless:
Every commercial product strives to claim a market niche. To this end, nearly every commercial smokeless product provides selections of tobaccos, processing methods, flavorants and humectants (nearly all proprietary secrets) to distinguish it from the products of its competitors.

At home, you can make your snuff, snus or chew any way you choose, and finely target your personal preference for texture, flavor, nicotine impact, etc. While many readers of this book are familiar with specific commercial products, and may find some satisfaction in replicating those, you may find an even greater satisfaction in creating your own, unique end product.

The recipes in this book are not definitive. Consider them a starting point for experimentation.

Containers and alkali: Stainless steel, ceramic, glass and some plastic containers are safe for mixing alkali solutions. Iron, aluminum and copper are not, and will leach metal into the solution.

Unit Conversion
(adapted from arizona.edu)

Length

1 inch (in or ") = 2.540 centimeters
1 millimeter (mm) = 0.03937 inches
1 foot (ft or ')= 30.4878 centimeters
1 centimeter (cm) = 0.3937 inches
1 yard (yd)= 0.9144028 meters
1 meter (m) = 3.281 feet

Area

1 square inch (sq. in. or in^2) = 6.4516 sq. centimeters
1 square centimeter (sq. cm. or cm^2) = 0.1550 sq. inches
1 square foot (sq. ft. or ft^2) = 0.0929 sq. meters (m

Weight

1 ounce (oz) = 28.3495 grams
1 gram (g) = 0.03527396 ounces
1 pound (lb) = 16 oz = 0.4535924 kilograms
1 kilogram (kg) = 2.2046223 pounds

Volume

1 teaspoon (tsp) = 5 milliliters
1 milliliter (ml) = 0.0338147 fluid ounces
1 centiliter (cl) = 10 milliliters
1 tablespoon (tbsp) = 3 tsp or 15 milliliters
1 liter (l) = 2.11342 pints = 1000 cubic centimeters = 10 deciliters (dl)
1 fluid ounce (oz) = 30 milliliters
1 liter (l) = 1.05671 quarts (qt) = 0.264178 gallons
1 gallon (gal) = 3.785332 liters = 231 cubic inches (cu. in. or in^3)
1 cup (c) = 0.23658 liters
1 pint (pt) = 0.473167 liters

Temperature

°Fahrenheit (°F): Subtract 32, then multiply by 5/9ths = °Celsius
°Celsius (°C): Multiply by 9/5ths, then add 32 = °Fahrenheit

Oral Snus

FmGrowit (2011): **Oral Snus**

Ingredients:

- 250 g (~½ pound) minced raw tobacco, fine or coarse according to preference and taste
- 0.4-0.5 l (13½-17 oz) water
- 55-70 g (~5-6½ tsp) non-iodized salt
- 10 g (~1 tsp) sodium carbonate
- 4-9 g (¾-1½ tsp) Glycerol
- Flavorings (essential oils, spirits, spices, etc.)

Method:

- Boil 4-5 dl water with non-iodized salt
- Let the salt water to cool to about 50°C (122°F)
- Using a stainless steel, glass or porcelain container able to withstand 75°C (~167°F), mix the salt water and tobacco
- Allow mixture to sit for 1 hour
- Stir the mixture thoroughly
- Cover the container with aluminum foil or lid
- Place the container in the oven, with a temperature of 55-75°C (131-167°F) for about **5 days**
- Stir contents of the container every day
- If the mixture becomes too dry, boil a cup water with 2 tsp salt, and blend in to the "right consistency" (taste & flavor).

[An alternative to the oven is to use a box of Styrofoam. For heat, use an incandescent light bulb, avoiding contact of the lamp with the

Styrofoam. You will have to experiment with the wattage of the light. Check the temperature with a thermometer inserted through the box roof.]

- After approximately 5 days, remove the container
- Mix the sodium carbonate in a little water, to dissolve
- With the container outdoors, mix the sodium carbonate solution into the tobacco
- Once the alkali reaction has subsided, thoroughly mix in Glycerol (1.5% -3.5%) of tobacco weight

Sodium carbonate is used to give the snus its characteristic flavor and aroma, which leads to a snus pH that is slightly alkaline.

You can now flavor your snus with pure essential oils. Such as rose, geranium and lemon oil, or even some tasty liquor varieties. Be careful, to experiment with a few drops at a time. The essential oil requires very small amounts, one or a few ml for 2 kg tobacco.

If the moisture content is too high, place the mixture on a newspaper covered with paper towels for final drying, 2-4 hours depending on season and room temperature.

You can now pack the snus into cans or boxes. Longer storage enhances the flavor. If you are not a large user, you can freeze the snus for a long time and always have access to fresh snus.

FmGrowit (2011): **Oral Snus Kit**
- Grind 1 kg tobacco (pipe tobacco like Caravelle) to a fine powder
- Mix tobacco powder with 1.1 l (~37 oz) water and 50 g (8⅓ tsp) salt
- Mix, spread out and cover
- Set the bowl to heat in 45-50°C for 5 days
- After five days, using a stainless steel, glass or ceramic container, mix in 90 g potassium carbonate (preferably outdoors)
- Work it thoroughly, and let it heat at 45-50°C for another 24 hours
- Stir so that it is evenly damp
- If you think that is too damp, one can fluff it and let it sit some hours uncovered
- When ready, pack in appropriate containers, and freeze most of the kit

When adding flavors, it is probably best to test them first in small amounts.   Juniper gives a taste similar to Gothenburg's rapé, bergamot oil compares to General.

justintempler (2011): **Oral Snus**
- The ratio of tobacco to water should be somewhere in the 1:1 to 1:1.5 range
- Salt should be 4-6 g per 100 g of dry tobacco (a lot of recipes have way too much salt)
- Sodium or potassium carbonate between 4 and 9 g per 100 g of dry tobacco.

You should not freeze snus until it has aged for a couple weeks in the fridge. Freezing it is an excellent method of storage but it needs to finish maturing in the refrigerator before freezing it. Freezing it stops the maturing process.

POGreen (2013): **Swedish Snus**

This is how I make 5½ Ibs of "Swedish Snus":
- 2¼ Ibs powdered tobacco (I use a meat grinder to grind my leaves
- 50 to 65 g of Salt [sodium chloride, or non-iodized table salt]
- 1.2 l OR 2½ pt of water

PRE-HEAT the oven to 194°F.
- Heat the water in a saucepan to lukewarm, take the pan off the stove, and pour the salt into the water. Dissolve it by stirring it until the water is clear.
- Have the tobacco powder in a bucket and pour the lukewarm salt solution over the powder. Mix together well.
- Use 2 heat-resistant, non-reactive [ceramic, glass or stainless] containers with a well-fitting lid on them to put the mixed tobacco powder in. Take a little at a time and give the powder a light pack all the way to the top.
- Make sure the containers can take 200°F in the oven.
- Bake at 194°F for 24 hours.
- Heat up 1½ pt water in a non-reactive saucepan [ceramic, glass or stainless] to lukewarm, take the pan off the stove, and pour in ~50 g of sodium carbonate. Dissolve it by stirring until clear.

DO THIS OUTSIDE!

- Take out the tobacco container(s) from the oven, pour the baked tobacco into a plastic bucket.
- Pour the sodium carbonate solution over the tobacco and mix with a plastic or stainless spoon.

MIX WELL
- Return the mixture to the heat resistant, non-reactive containers, cover, and return to the oven at 194°F for another 12 hours.
- Remove from the oven, and allow to cool with THE LID ON. Once cooled to about room temperature, store it in the fridge.

The longer you keep it in the fridge, the better.

Referring to the above recipe, beware of using too much of the sodium carbonate, as it can affect your gums. Rather use a strong tobacco instead of using too much sodium carbonate.

COMMENTS:
squeezyjohn:
salt brine: usually 6-10 g of dry salt (sodium chloride) per 100 g of tobacco dissolved in 100 to 160 ml of water (it depends on how absorbent the tobacco is).

DGBAMA (2014): Mint / Menthol Oral Snus

1 lb batch: with menthol crystals, a little goes a long way. An easy menthol casing is 1 oz vodka and ¼ tsp crystals, which dissolve easily. Start with a small amount and adjust to taste, you can always add, cannot take away. Put it in a fine mist sprayer and spray a few times, then let it rest and absorb at least 12 hours. Try it, and if not enough, repeat the process. When you like it, use the total number of sprays on the next batch.

COMMENTS:
squeezyhohn:
With snus (a regular plain snus recipe of tobacco, water, salt, and sodium or potassium carbonate), add the flavourings *afterwards*. I would tend towards a lighter flavoured tobacco base for a minty one, and maybe add a little sweetness in the original snus by adding a little xylitol or root liquorice powder in the beginning of the recipe. For flavouring, I would use a mix of peppermint and spearmint oils, with a little menthol crystals diluted in alcohol.

squeezyjohn (2014): Snus from Silver River

I've just made my first batch of snus from the Silver River I grew this year, and I am in love with the taste already!

As a test of it's flavour potential I made this batch simply from
- 100 g tobacco flour (lamina only, with no stems)
- 8 g salt (sodium chloride)
- 120 ml water
- potassium carbonate

by my normal method of cooking at 85°C for 2 days.

[see squeezyjohn's Recipe for Ettan Snus, and leave out the cocoa.]

It comes out with no bitterness and a very bright, balanced flavour, with a lovely incense-like resin aroma, almost like it is flavoured with essential oils (none were added at all). I think this is the same thing about this tobacco which makes people smoking it suggest it is menthol flavoured. The taste for me is very similar to a kind of snus from Northern Sweden I used to be able to get, called Gellivare. It is really very nice indeed! The nicotine strength of this snus is not too strong, just regular.

The surprising thing is that this snus did not need very much aging at all to taste very nice. Often you have to leave the snus to rest for 3 weeks to let the flavour develop, but this one tastes great within days.

So the verdict on Silver River is a massive thumbs up from me: easy to grow, huge yields, magnificent looking plants, nice snus. I couldn't wish for more. If blended with a darker tasting variety of tobacco for a richer snus I imagine it would also be great.

I managed to get 3 kg of flour from 18 Silver River plants! I had to get rid of the stems because they were beginning to mould. So that weight is lamina only! Very productive!

It is normal I think for making snus to use the whole leaf, stems and all (but not the stalk). I tend to use lamina only in my recipes as I like a strong snus and a smooth grind. But some varieties I grind the stems too. Stems absorb more moisture and give the snus a nice texture.

Yes the yield is higher than I first thought. The plants grew very big even without much extra feeding and watering by me throughout the season. They had a spacing of about 80 cm between plants in a staggered grid, and although they ended up touching each other, the leaves got enough sunlight that there was a good nicotine level from the middle leaves up.

[After two months it] has mellowed out very nicely now, and has a deep, earthy taste, with a little of the incense/herbal note still there. I might sweeten my next batch with a little liquorice as this air cured tobacco has no natural sweetness left in it. To me it has just the right amount of nicotine in it.

kullas (2015): Dip
- ¾ qt bone dry tobacco
- ½ c soy sauce
- 1 tbsp molasses
- 1 tbsp baking powder
- 1 tsp honey
- 1 tsp liquid smoke
- ½ tsp salt
- 1 tsp concentrated flavor vanilla, mint etc.

The texture of it through the metal mesh kitchen strainer gets real close.
- bring all ingredients but tobacco to a short boil and mix well with tobacco.

If after mixing, there is extra juice, ether add more tobacco or pour it off.

If there is not enough juice, you can add ether a tad more soy or plain water.

COMMENTS:
jaysalti (2016)
Baking was only used to dry the leaves and stems. Recommended to grind stems separate to allow for better control of consistency.

_____

jojjas (2014): Latakia Snus
- Flour of 200 g (~7 oz) WLT Latakia
- 300 g (10½ oz) half my own and half WLT Izmir
- 0.8 l water
- 100 g (3½ oz) salt

120 hours in 95°C (203°F)

And how does it taste then? Awesome according to my preference. I think it tastes just like a real smoky, Scottish single malt, like Ardbeg or Lagavulin, just awesome

COMMENTS:
POGreen (2014)
I add the potash or sodium carbonate AFTER the heat process and then let it rest for about 2 weeks in the fridge.
I use 15-20 g of potash (potassium carbonate) to 500 g of flour.
A friend of mine got himself a pressure cooker. According to him he can reduce that week in the oven into 8 effective hours and have the same quality, a major difference.
After 2 weeks in the fridge I start using the snus and it tastes good; after 2 months it is indescribably great.
Leaf I have used for snus:
- VA 309 Fire-cured
- Dark Air-cured
- Small Stalk Black Mammoth
- Flue-cured Virginia Red
- Piloto Cubano Viso
- Brazilian Mata Fina

_____

squeezyjohn (2014): Tobacco Varieties for Oral Snus

Bright leaf (flue cured): Makes a nice balanced, medium strength snus if I use only the lamina part of the whole leaf. It seems a bit weak if I include ground stems. This leaf seems to grind up nice and fine, which gives the snus a nice texture. The aroma of this leaf comes through a little, but it is muted compared to the smell of the leaves themselves. There is a little residual sweetness, and it's nice mild, balanced flavour.

Red leaf Virginia: I find this makes a very harsh tasting snus, even after lots of aging—at least using my process it does!

Burley: This snus is very, very strong, if made purely with [WLT] burley. I get around this by using a bit less potash in the recipe. It gives off much more ammonia in the process, and so needs a longer aging time. However after aging, it is rich, dark and chocolaty, and of a pretty high nicotine strength.

Fire-cured VA: An experimental batch of snus using 100% fire-cured showed that it is far too smokey to make a nice snus. My technique of making snus seems to change the smokey chemicals into a kind of burnt rubber taste, and it was unusable. In fact, any blend in which I have used this in quantities of over 5%, have been unusable, due to this flavour change.

Izmir: Makes a snus that smells deliciously aromatic, but has little or no nicotine content to it, and it is a bit bitter. As such I only ever think about using it to cut the nicotine down in a strong tobacco blend, or as a flavouring ingredient.

Dark air-cured ligero (3rd priming): This makes a high nicotine snus which is very bitter indeed. If it wasn't for this bitterness, then the lovely cigar like properties that come through the making process would be a fantastic taste. But as it is, even 10% in a blend will render any snus I make quite bitter.

After you make the snus there is not a point in even trying it for 3 weeks after it is made, as it will taste horrible! Longer aging smooths out the flavours more.

squeezyjohn (2017): Julesnus clone

Grog is an old British Navy term for a drink of watered down rum, and has been extrapolated to mean any strong drink. However I can see where the confusion lies. Julesnus is supposed to taste like the Swedish Christmas drink called "Glögg". Glögg is very similar to mulled wine— red wine heated up with whole spices and citrus peels, sometimes fortified with extra brandy or aquavit.

The key to success with flavours was to produce the snus from the tobacco and then add just the right blend of very high quality natural flavouring extracts. However if trying to make it at home I would probably not use extracts or oils as they're very hard to get the right dose for a small batch.

To replicate the flavour at home might require a bit of experimentation. My suggestion would be to try and produce a fairly light tasting snus from tobaccos that are not too dark and rich, replace some of the water in the recipe with red wine, then add ground spices AFTER THE COOK. My experience of adding aromatic ground spices is that the aroma tends to evaporate off if added before cooking.

The traditional spices in Glögg are: Cinnamon, cardamom, clove, ginger and orange peel. I would personally take the cooked snus after it has cooled down, add the finely ground spices carefully a little at a time and mix in well before tasting. Taste it, bearing in mind that the snus has not aged at all. From smelling my can of Julesnus, I reckon the main spices are cinnamon, cardamom and clove (in that order). A few weeks of aging will help the spices go right through the blend.

COMMENT:
...created a snus which is awfully close to Julesnus. For 80 grams of tobacco, 24 sprays of the Watkins orange extract, along with ⅛ tsp of the following spice recipe:
- 6 parts cinnamon
- 3 parts cardamom
- 1 part clove

a discussion (2017): Oral Snus—reducing bitterness

Dark tobacco varieties tend to be more bitter than burley or Maryland. Stems contain lower levels of nicotine than their lamina. Stems are also used to reduce bitterness. Stems must be totally dried, then ground to the desired texture.

With home-grown leaf, seasonal variations in weather and soil conditions may affect the degree of bitterness in the harvested leaf. Longer cooking times tend to reduce bitterness. Resting time (measured in weeks) in the refrigerator tends to reduce bitterness.

---

a discussion (2017): Modern production of Swedish snus

"A blend of leaf tobaccos is ground and sieved to specified particle sizes. The ground tobacco is mixed with water and sodium chloride [table salt] in closed process blenders. The mixture is then subjected to a computer-controlled heat-treatment process, the purpose of which is to improve the taste and to reduce microbial activity to obtain a proper shelf life. The heating is achieved by using hot water and by injecting steam into the blenders. It involves temperatures up to 80-100 degrees centigrade during several hours. Finally the snus is cooled and other ingredients such as flavors and humectants [polypropylene and/or glycerin] are added before the finished product is fed to automatic packers.

Retailers are encouraged to keep the snus refrigerated in order to meet the criteria for the 'best-before' labeling. However, there is no need for a completely uninterrupted cool chain as the low bacterial activity in the product implies stability also at room temperature."

LE Rutqvist,M Curvall T Hassler, T. Ringberger, I Wahlberg. Swedish snus and the GothiaTek® standard. Harm Reduct J. 2011; 8:11.

COMMENTS:

squeezyjohn (2014):

I make my snus with a temperature of 85°C for 48 hours. I find that with higher temperatures my snus becomes "burnt" tasting. With good hygiene and the addition of 8 g salt to 100 g tobacco flour this seems to be fine for killing mould and bacteria. When the snus is aged for a week and the funky ammonia smell dissipates, then I freeze it until I want to use it, which stops the growth of anything again.

SmokesAhoy (2017):

I'll chime in here. I pressure cook it for 4 hours with salt, flour and water. Then I mix in alkali, 1 additional hour of cooking, and let it cool down gradually on the stove. When cold next day, I add a bit licorice and vegetable glycerin, and let it age with a paper towel held in place by the jar ring. I use more water in the cook than is the norm, so it dries up and off gasses at the same time. Ready in 2 weeks.

Copenhagen Forever (2016): "Gold" Oral Snus

- Cut up the stems, veins and leaf. and keep separate.
- Dry well in the oven at 275°F.
- Stems grinding: three 10 second burst will do.

Dump it out on a paper plate and tap from the bottom. All the big stuff will come to the top. Pick out the big ones to regrind. Dump the flour in a plastic bag.

- Veins get three 2 second burst and that usually does it.
- Leaf grinds quickly: three ½ second bursts, and it's done.
- This cook is going to be with 10 oz of dry tobacco.

The formula:

- 8 oz tobacco
- 1 c water
- 1 tbsp sea salt

I make extra solution and go by feel as to how wet the tobacco is. The above ingredients end up a bit dry. I'll have extra solution and get it a little wetter. 3 c water and 3 tbsp sea salt will be plenty. The last tbsp is a bit shy of full because I want it a little less salty.

- Bring it to a boil to dissolve the salt.

I can add at least ⅔ of the solution and then adjust it from there. It's probably 40% water by weight to start the cooking. I add just plain water every time I take it out to stir it, every day.

Pack the jars with your fingers, and clean off the rim so it will seal. Screw on the lid, and snug it.

I bought a cheap Crockpot, and bought the wrong one. This one only has low and high. A dimmer switch works to keep the temp where I want it. I have the jars in, and they float. I was going to weigh them down, but forgot on my last batch. When I stirred them I found that they were cooking evenly so I didn't bother with it.

Kinds of Crockpots: Buy what you can. The ones with a warm setting will sit at 170°F. You can cover them to raise the temp, using tin foil or a blanket. The dimmer wires up easily with the little wiring diagram they give you. This one is rated at 600 amps. The Crockpot was $13 at Walmart, and the dimmer was $5.

I fill the crock ¾ full of hot tap water, put in the jars which sit about a ½" below the lid. I plug the Crockpot straight into a socket with a GFI [ground fault interruption], then turn it on high. Since the dimmer gets warm when using it to initially heat up the lot, I plug the Crockpot straight in. It warms at 5°F every 10 minutes. I want 190°F steady on this cook. Between 180 and 200°F is perfect.

Now I shut off the Crockpot, plug in the dimmer, and turn the Crockpot back on high. I now control the Crockpot with the dimmer. I've already used it to cook, and marked where my desired temps are at. I cooked this batch for 72 hours. It reached temperature at 4:30 pm here, so tomorrow at 4:30 will be the first time I stir. The temperature stayed at 190°F for 24 hours. I get some evaporation. As the water level drops, the temp rises. The water didn't drop more than a ¼" but the temp went up by 2°F. I use leather gloves and a big spoon to get the jars out. There is some pressure when I open the jars. Sounds like a soda can opening.

The snus has a nice color now. I add a ½ cup of water, and it's still pretty dry. I guess it's suppose to stay dry thru the cooking. I read it somewhere and haven't tried cooking it any wetter than about 40%.

It's a dark cocoa brown before the alkali goes in. All the rest of my ingredients make a slurry stirred up. I keep it suspended in the bowl and splash it over the top of the tobacco.

After mixing, remove jar lid, and replace with a paper coffee filter beneath the jar's ring.

The recipe for the black gold in question is based on a small, 8 oz. batch.
- 6 oz BigBonners Burly (older)
- 1 oz BigBonners Dark air-cured (older)
- 1 oz Dark fire-cured (old left over, probably 6 years old)
- 1 c water
- 1 tbsp Sea salt
- Cook at 180-200°F for 72 hours

Adding alkali:
- Mix in a little bowl
- 2-3 tbsp water or as needed
- 1 tsp Bakers Ammonia
- 2 tbsp Sodium Carbonate (baking soda converted)
- 2 tsp Glycerin (or more, until the tobacco is clumping)
- Stir it well
- Let it breath for 2 weeks, stirring at 1 week, and adding water.
- I vacuum sealed and froze all.

_____

Snusser (2016): Oral Snus
- 50 g Virginia Red Leaf, dried, ground and sifted into flour
- 100 g All Natural Burley, dried, ground, and sifted into flour
- 14 g Salt
- 125 g Water
- 24 hours @ 85°C, in a glass canning jar
- Remove from heat
- Place snus in mixing bowl
- 14 g sodium carbonate, added dry. Stir very well
- Place snus back in glass jar
- 12 hours @ 85°C

When the sodium carbonate is added, the stuff is unfit for polite company for a week or two at least.

COMMENTS:

squeezyjohn (2016): Grinding is more time-efficient if you do it in large batches, and store your leaf as tobacco flour. It takes up far less space that way too!

When you add the alkali, it's like a cross between a dirty men's room in a stinking bar and a baby's diaper, but give it a few weeks and then it's a whole different ball game.

SmokesAhoy (2016): Pressure Cooker Snus
[1 pound of whole leaf makes about 1 quart of tobacco flour without the stems.]
- 65 g tobacco flour
- 75 g water
- 5 g glycerin
- 6.5 g salt
- Place well-mixed ingredients in a canning jar, then seal with a canning lid.
- Cook at pressure for 4 hours.
- Add 6.5 g washing soda dissolved in 1 tbsp hot water, and mix

thoroughly.
- Return to the pressure cooker and cook at pressure for an additional hour.
- Remove jar from the cooker, and allow to cool.
- Remove lid, replace lid with a coffee filter, and screw in place with rim.
- Mix it periodically for several days, then seal it. Allow it to rest.

[Totally comparable product to the low and slow method, after resting for 1 month.]

ALTERNATIVE with stems:
- 25 g lamina, 20 g rib, total 45 g
- 4 g salt
- 3 g glycerin
- 45 g water
- Mix non tobacco ingredients until totally incorporated into hot water.
- Incorporate the resulting water mix totally into tobacco.
- Next into pressure cooker for 5 hours.
- Add 4 g washing soda to 12 g hot water, allow to go into solution entirely.
- Mix into cooked flour thoroughly, return to pressure for 1 hour.

COMMENTS:

squeezyjohn (2017):

I have done side-by-side batches of identical snus cooked until it darkens sufficiently at different temperatures using the *sous vide* machine.
- 60°C for 7 days
- 70°C for 4 days
- 80°C for 2 days
- 90°C for 24 hours
- 100°C for 6 hours (hard to control as the water was boiling the whole time and needed replacing)

My results were snuses of increasing darkness with increasing temperature. A richness of flavour and caramelization also increased while the more delicate aromas (chocolate, honey, vanilla tones) decreased with increasing temperature. The 60°C version lacked body and had a malty, mealy taste while the 100°C version lacked aroma and seemed slightly bitter. Since doing that experiment I have settled on temperatures in the 75-85°C range for all my cooks with a cook time at between 1 and 3 days using the *sous vide* machine.

manstrom (2019): Improvised Dip

Having a preference for fine cut I do a 25:75 mix of cigar tobacco and Camel cigarette tobacco, and pulse in my extra coffee grinder. Pack tightly in a jar. The sauce mix is soy sauce with salt added to taste. Keep it at a strong simmer for 6-7 hours. About midway, add Sodium Carbonate at this stage. Carry the bottle outside to avoid killing everyone with the freshly opened ammonia smell, and transfer it for a 4-5 day stint before canning. Add in vegetable glycerin.

jParnell (2020): Gourmet Artisanal Spittin' Dip

Ingredients:
- Tobacco: 120 g after drying
- Distilled water:~150 ml
- Kosher salt: ~21.5 g
- Glycerin (food grade): ~15.5 ml
- Propylene Glycol (food grade): ~8 ml
- Sodium Carbonate: 8 g (range 6 g to 12 g)
- Flavoring as desired. I add natural flavoring (i.e., licorice root, cinnamon sticks, anything from the spice cabinet, etc.), *before* cooking, and add extracts or essential oils *after* cooking.

Preparation:
- Shred or grind tobacco, and completely dry it (for weighing)
- Re-dry and re-grind the stems if still too coarse
- Place dry tobacco flour into Mason jars, to about ⅓-full
- In a separate container, bring the water to near a boil, and dissolve in the salt

- Pour the salt solution into the tobacco flour in each jar, adding just enough to reach half-way up the jar
- Fluff the wet tobacco mixture with a fork
- Seal the lids onto the jars with a gentle tightening of the ring
- I cook mine at 185°F (85°C) for 24 hours. Every 3-6 hours, I remove the jars from heat, remove the lids, and thoroughly mix with a fork so that everything is cooked more evenly.

[I use a sous-vide cooker set to run no higher than 185°F (85°C). Times and temps vary depending on the type of tobacco and the outcome you're looking for. At 185°F (85°C), you may need only 24 hours, but at 130°F (55°C) it can take up to a week. The tobacco is done when it has reached a rich, dark chocolate brown, similar to used dark roast coffee.]

- Dissolve the sodium carbonate in a small amount of hot water (in a non-reactive container), then [preferably outdoors] divide the solution equally into the jars of tobacco flour. *[Allow it to mostly out-gas, before bringing back indoors.]*
- Add essential oils or flavor extracts at this point
- Cover the jars using a piece of coffee filter in place of the jar lid, and hold it in place with the ring.
- I now place mine into the refrigerator to complete the out-gassing
- Tasting a pinch weekly allows me to determine when it is ready for use. When there is little or no change from one tasting to the next (typically after 2 to 3 weeks), then it can be portioned into smaller containers, and stored in the fridge or freezer.

Ifyougotem (2020): DIY Dip Pouch from Coffee Filter

Wrap little burritos using a square cut from a coffee filter. Work's great, you can customize the size, and plenty cheap.

---

squeezyjohn (2013): "Ettan" Oral Snus   ◀◀◀
Making tobacco flour:
The first thing you must do is strip the midribs from the leaf just like for cigarettes. But when making snus, retain the stems in a separate pile.

You have to grind the leaf in to flour. Any grinding technique will work, but make sure the leaf is fully dried out in the oven or the sun so that it is crispy and completely moisture free before grinding. My technique of grinding, which is good for fairly large batches, is to crunch the leaves so they shatter to tiny fragments and then blitz this is a food processor or blender until a fine powder is obtained. Tobacco flour can be stored long term in this form in a sealed glass jar. I keep separate jars for the leaf lamina flour and the stem flour. Stem flour is lower flavour and nicotine but, can be used to balance out stronger tobaccos.

Lye Water:
The only other ingredient you need that is not a common store cupboard ingredient is lye water, which is available as a food grade additive from Chinese/Far-Eastern supermarkets. It's usually used in the production of noodles. Lye water is a concentrated potassium carbonate solution, and it's used as an alkali to increase the potency of the snus. [The lye water I use in my recipes is a 42% by weight potassium carbonate solution.]

Equipment needed:
CROCKPOT / SLOW COOKER
To successfully make the snus you need a method of keeping the mix at a constant temperature for long periods of time. I use the cheapest available •Crockpot. This will be used as a water bath. I also made a trivet from bent chicken wire fencing to keep any contents of the water bath from sitting right on the bottom of the Crockpot.
PID TEMPERATURE CONTROL UNIT
Crockpots alone do not give a constant controllable temperature, so I also bought a PID unit designed to convert a Crockpot in to a *sous-vide* machine cheaply. A quick google will find plenty of these devices

available. You simply plug the PID into the mains electricity, plug the slow cooker in to the PID, insert the temperature probe into the crock pot filled with water, close the lid, and set the temperature to maintain on the PID unit. Anything now placed in the water bath will be maintained at that temperature. *[The Crockpot must have an analog (dial) switch, since digital Crockpots may not come back on after the power is cut off by the PID.]*

KILNER / MASON JARS

Any water tight, sealed container which will fit inside the Crockpot water bath will do, but I like Kilner clip top jars with a rubber seal as the glass is inert, they're long lasting (provided you don't shock them with heat—they shatter then!). Make sure that they will fit inside the Crockpot.

The **recipe** yields about 10 regular cans or 500 g (~1 lb) of loose snus:
- 100 g (3½ oz) Virginia Bright Leaf Lamina Flour
- 100 g (3½ oz) Burley Lamina Flour
- 1 tsp cocoa powder
- 16 g (½ oz) sea salt
- 240 ml (8 fl oz) boiled water

Method:
- The tobacco flours and cocoa powder were combined and mixed thoroughly.
- The salt was dissolved in the water, and then mixed with the tobacco flours and cocoa powder mix using a food processor to get a thorough mixing. However a fork and a bowl is a fine way to mix.
- The mixture was turned in to a 0.5 l Kilner jar, sealed with the rubber ring to ensure water-tightness and was then heated to 85°C (185°F) and held at that temperature for 24 hours in the Crockpot water bath.
- After this first cook, 5 tsp of lye water was added, and mixed in thoroughly. This was then put back in the Crockpot for another 12 hours at a cooler temperature of 75°C (167°F).
- Remove the jar from the crock pot, and leave in a cool place for 5 days with the rubber seal removed to allow ammonia gas

which can spoil the flavour to de-gas.

The resulting snus is a perfect copy of Ettan, the oldest brand of Swedish snus still available today. It is rich, chocolaty and tobacco flavoured, and this recipe makes a regular strength snus of about 8 mg/g nicotine.

The snus can then be stored for a month refrigerated in whatever container is available, provided it's airtight. For longer keeping of up to a year, the snus can be frozen with no ill effects.

If you are a user of portion snus then it is possible to turn this loose snus in to the small pouches by buying these things called Prillan Portionspasars. It's a fiddly process though. You have to cut the end from a small syringe and force the snus in to it and then inject each individual bag, and heat-seal the open end. When I make portions I use hair straighteners to seal the end! However if the idea of using hair-straighteners challenges your masculinity, you can use a soldering iron. It's always better to add most flavourings after the cooking process.

COMMENTS:

jojjas (2013):

the old method to make snus is following

Mix all ingredients together and place it in heat source for 120 hours in 50°-55°C (122-131°F)

squeezyjohn (2013):

The traditional way of taking it in Sweden is to form a small pellet slightly smaller than a marble and place it in the upper lip towards the front of the mouth. Then you need to relax and leave it alone, which takes a lot of practice.

dubhelix (2014):

I made a small batch of snus using elements from squeezyjohn's recipe. The ingredients were as follows:

- 40 g powdered leaf (mostly Small Stalk Black Mammoth, with a bit of Virginia Bright Leaf and some Yellow Twist Bud)

- 80 g water (probably a little too much)
- 8 g NaCl (table salt)
- 1.3 g K2CO3 (potassium carbonate)
- 4 drops Almond Extract
- ¼ tsp cocoa

Tobacco, salt and 60g water cooked at 90°C in mason jar in Crockpot water bath for about 24 hours, K2CO3 dissolved in 20 g of water, mixed well, added flavorings, cooked again for 24 hours. Yielded 132 g of snus, packed into three 44 g cans.

squeezyjohn (2016): All Bolivian Criollo Black [BCB]
I did my BCB single strain snus at 75°C rather than my usual 85°C for 3 days cooking time. I'm currently loving the batch I made with 100% home grown Bolivian Criollo Black. It was a 100 g tobacco flour recipe with no added flavourings apart from salt, and I added just 2 drops of pure bergamot oil and mixed, once it was finished. It's had 3 weeks of age after cooking and it's a real close a General clone: absolutely delicious, and packs a punch. And the best thing is that this one is just HOME-GROWN!!! Woohoo!

Ozzy (2021):
Just finished flavoring an Ettan inspired recipe:
- 100 mg burley
- 100 mg water
- 10 mg salt

Instant pot Pressure cooked for two hours, kept warm for two more.
- 5 mg sodium carbonate dissolved in 10 mg water
- Mixed for an hour to release gases

Flavoring:
- 15 mg cacao 100%
- 2 mg caramel flavor
- 1 mg vanilla extract
- 10 mg vegetable glycerin

I am very happy the way it turned out.

_____

wruk53 (2021): **Oral Snus**

- tobacco 100 g
- water 66 g
- salt (non-iodized table salt) 5-8 g
- sodium carbonate 5-8 g

I use @squeezyjohn's method. I've made several batches using this method. I use a Crockpot and Mason jars for the cooking. I recommend using a mix of dark air cured and MD609 for my tobaccos. The dark air cured is very high in nicotine and the MD adds good flavor. I measure all my components by weight instead of a combination of weight and volume. For example, if I use 100 g of tobacco I use about 66 g of water instead of a volume of water. This will seem pretty dry when you mix it up, but it will cook up fine and you can add more water later if needed. For each 100 g of tobacco, use a range from 5 g to 8 g of salt and 5 g to 8 g of sodium carbonate. My slow cooker maintains a pretty constant temp of about 185 to 190°F on low setting. Make a small batch first and correct your mistakes the next time if needed. By the way, don't try the pressure cooker method, it cooks the tobacco to a mush.

If your leaf was ripe when picked, if it was color cured and dried properly and, last but not least, if it was aged long enough, it does not have to be [additionally] fermented. If you can answer yes to all those things, you should be good to go.

billy (2021): **Unflavored Oral Snus**

50 g of dark air cure from WLT ground in a NutriBullet blender, 50 g hot water with 5 g salt in it, mixed together. Lightly packed in jar and sealed. Into pressure cooker for 4 hrs. Back in mixing bowl. 3.5 g sodium carbonate mixed with enough hot water to dissolve it and 20 drops glycerin all mixed and cooked another 1 hr. Mixed around and let breath off ammonia.

Tobaccofieldsforever (2021): **My Dad's Oral Snus**

My dad just hand wrote this on a piece of paper for me to share with this forum. It is very similar to squeezyjohn's recipe in many ways, if you would like to reference that as well.

Ingredients:
- 4 c tobacco flour
- 2½ c hot water (non-chlorinated)
- 2 tbsp non-iodized salt
- 2 tbsp sodium carbonate

Dissolve salt in hot water. Pour over tobacco flour and mix until tobacco is totally moistened. Transfer mixture to a Crockpot WITH A LID, set on warm mode (Crockpot must have "warm" setting). My dad uses a 2-quart size which holds the 4 c perfectly. Put lid on and leave for AT LEAST 24 hours, but mixture will not be damaged if left for longer. (He said he has left it for up to 3 days with similar results.) Dump mixture into mixing bowl, and add sodium carbonate. Stir well. Return mixture to Crockpot on "warm" setting, put lid back on, and let it go another 24 hours.

Dump mixture into mixing bowl, and stir every 10 minutes or so until ammonia smell completely dissipates into air. This should take about half an hour or a little longer. Snus is now finished and ready for use. Transfer the finished product into container with lid, and store in refrigerator. Fill your tins from this as needed. This size batch will generally last my dad 2 to 3 weeks. He has made several batches ahead of time and frozen them in Ziploc freezer bags with great success.

SIDE NOTE: The amount of water needed can depend on type of tobacco and what it takes for your tobacco to appear "completely moistened". My dad uses a tobacco he has been growing for 20 years that was developed by a commercial tobacco farmer in Maryland for his "personal stock" It was crossed with Yellow Orinoco 9 the first year growing it and has been growing true many years now. It seems like a Maryland / burley variety though it has some Virginia characteristics. It is smooth smoking by itself and makes a nice snus as well.

—————————

Robncars (2020): Oral Dip

- Approximately 2 lbs tobacco flour (was 3 lbs whole leaves)
- 4- 12 oz apple juice
- 12 oz water
- 1 c glycerin
- 1 c salt (I use pink Himalayan)
- 4 tbsp cumin

Bring juice to a boil, lower heat, but hold boil. Slowly mix in water, glycerin, salt and cumin, mixing well. Pour into Crockpot (set to high). Add tobacco slowly, mixing well, then plug Crockpot into a temp controller. Hold at 165°F for 24 hrs.

COMMENTS:

ArizonaDave (2021)

A few years back, I took all my dark air scraps (dried) and ground it into a powder, then used a metal strainer to remove stems. All that was left was powder. I have around 4 pounds of this stuff for an emergency, and for experiments. The best mix was a rum/vanilla re-dried, which can be used dry or re-moisturized. The dark air has a natural raisin flavor.

_____

Cray Squirrel (2021): K.I.S.S. Oral Dip

KISS Base Dip recipe

- 100 g tobacco (I use burley, fire-cured dark tobacco, or a mix).
- 10 g salt. NaCl
- 7 g licorice root powder for fuller flavor (and at this amount wont taste like candy)
- 7 to 10 g sodium carbonate (depending on tobacco)
- 110 g water. Tap water is fine unless you have very heavily mineralized water.
- 5 g Food grade glycerin (3 to 7 g range) for mouth feel, sweetening and to keep it moist. (humectant and preservative)

Leaf is oven dried a couple hours. Run the whole leaf into a blender or food processor until fine, then run through a screen to remove larger pieces of tobacco stems.

- Heat water and dissolve salt, glycerin, sodium carbonate and licorice powder.
- Add tobacco and mix well. If the tobacco isn't moist appearing, not wet, add a bit more water. Dry tobacco will not cook evenly.
- Cook in pressure cooker in sealed jars or oven bags for 2-3 hours at 15 psi. If using an oven, place jars in a pan of water at 250°F. This will give same sterilizing temperature.
- Allow to cool, then stir open jars a few times a day sitting on counter.
- Any flavorings (casings) can be added at this time. Wintergreen, mint apple, citrus etc.
- After a few days it's ready to use.

This is my go to, base recipe. I am still experimenting, but it has wonderful texture and taste. I smoke-cure my color-cured leaf, in high case with mesquite pellets for great, to me, taste. Hickory, oak or any common wood used for smoking would work.

Tobacco I am using and have grown is Madole, Little Yellow and Black Mammoth as dark air/fire-cured types, many burleys, and a few Virginias. Dark air-cured tobaccos are the best for dip, because of their high nicotine, leaf weight and substance. Burleys are lower in nicotine but still are plenty high for good dip. Virginias does not have a high nicotine level, but I am experimenting with them for taste blending.

- 100 g batch of tobacco flour yields 280 g finished dip
- Each can of commercial dip contains 35 g dipping tobacco
- Each 100 g batch yields the equivalent of 8 cans dip

It usually takes 3 days to sweeten the smell, but taste is good by next morning, and very good in 3 days. Nicotine levels seem higher than commercial. Texture isn't the same, unless you cook it a long time and break down the fibers. It pinches and holds together perfectly, and doesn't dry out with the food grade glycerin. Moisture level has gotten easier to adjust after a few batches. Just make sure when you mix dry tobacco flour with the wet ingredients that you aren't afraid to add a few ounces of water beyond the 110 g initially added. The smokiness will come thru subtly after a couple days.

COMMENTS:
wruk53 (2021)
This is almost the same way I make snus, except I slow cook mine in sealed jars in a water bath and I don't use quite as much water. Also, I don't put the sodium carbonate in for the first cook. I cook it for about 30 hours at 175°F, then mix in the alkali, and cook another 12 hours. You can always add more water later if needed. This method always turns out a good product if the tobacco used is of good quality.

_____

Ozzy (2021): Wet Extra Stark Mynta Oral Snus

- 50 g Mint Virginia (Wintergreen/Yellow Virginia)
- 25 g Yellow Virginia
- 25 g Red Burley Tobacco
- 10 g salt
- 100 g water
- 8.7 g sodium carbonate diluted in 10 g of additional water
- Base Flavor 10g = 5 g spearmint + 2 g vanilla +1 g caramel
- Middle Flavor 7 g = 2 g sage + 2 g chocolate + 1 g anisette + 2g patchouli
- End Flavor 12 ml = 10 ml peppermint + 2 ml black pepper**
- 5 g glycerin for stabilizing

I milled the tobacco to a fine flour to pack in portions.

- I pressure sterilized the solutions in a slow cooker bag in an instant pot cooker for two hours under pressure and two hours under heated pressure release.
- I mixed for half an hour for ammonia release and left it covered for the next day.
- I finished doing the flavor additions and filled six tins (about 110 portions) and refrigerated the rest.

Please notice that the End Flavors are measured in **ml not weight **because of the different density**.

This is such a complex and flavorful wallop of mints and notes. It pleasantly stings in the gums and fills your mouth and sinuses with a fresh minty feeling. It is a definitely an amazing combination with a diverse bouquet of harmonious flavors.

The patchouli used was a little sketchy, and the middle flavor addition had an additional botanical aroma, but when blended, it subsided and the patchouli notes remained. Peppermint extract: next time I will use 5-6 ml.

Some may enjoy making a more coarse tobacco flour, probably 50% milled and 50% long cut, the current mixture immediately delivers a strong yet constant nicotine release. I love the way my current formula delivers a strong impact in flavor and nicotine (Siberia like) but some might like to tone it down.

_____

wruk53 (2021): Dark Air-Cured and Katerini Oral Snus

80% dark air-cured and 20% Katerini. I used the Squeezyjohn water bath method, and once again it turned out really good. I used my instant pot this time on the *low warm* setting. It maintained a temp of 176°F on that setting, so I cooked it 45 hours for the initial cook and 10 hours for the alkalizing cook. I tested my pot on the *slow cook* settings first and they were all too hot. The instant pot automatically shuts itself off after 10 hours on the warm setting, so you have to periodically turn it off and restart it. Not a big deal for me, I'm retired and stay home most of the time anyway. Proportions used were:

- 240 g of dark air-cured
- 60 g of Katerini flours
- about 200 g of water (hydrated at 66%)
- 21 g of salt
- 21 g of sodium carbonate mixed with about 40 g of water for the second cook.

It was a little bit bitter, so I added a small amount of mulethi powder (licorice root) to balance it out and provide some sweetness.

_____

wruk53 (2022): **Small Stalk Black Mammoth Oral Snus**

Started a batch of Snus this morning. I used
- 400 g Small Stalk Black Mammoth (SSBM) flour
- 260 g water
- 24 g salt
- 24 g sodium carbonate

I'll cook it for 30 hours at 176°F, then alkalize with the sodium carbonate mixed in about 100g of water, and cook another 12 hours at the same temperature. After that, it's into the fridge for aging/degassing for at least 2 weeks. At that point, after tasting, I may or may not add some mulethi (licorice root) powder to counteract any bitterness, if needed. Then it will be divided up into 3 ounce batches, put in Ziploc snack bags, wrapped in foil and frozen.

The tobacco was from my spring crop. It was kilned for 6 weeks and smells fantastic.

Total cook time was about 44 hours. It takes about 2 to 3 weeks in the fridge before it reaches its peak taste and smoothness. I alkalized it yesterday, and it gave off the nose burning, eye watering fumes that indicate high ammonia content.

My Snus has been in the fridge for 13 days now. I've been sampling it for the last few days. The nicotine content is high. It has a spicy sort of taste and is very bitter. I had to add quite a bit of mulethi powder to offset the bitterness. The SSBM is one that definitely needs to be blended with a milder variety. It's usable though, as is. Next time I'll try a 50/50 blend of SSBM/Shirazi. Some of the bitterness may be because of the high nicotine content. Alkaloids are generally bitter.

After 4 weeks, the snus improved with age. I think I would classify it as good to very good at this point. I've had to reduce my portion size by about half due to the very high nicotine content.

I never measure the amounts of flavoring agents. I just go by taste a little at a time. I guesstimate about 15 to 20 g of mulethi (licorice root) powder added to about 500 g of snus, mixed in well.

Jitterbugdude (2019): **Brief Description of How I Make Dip**

1. Pack a mason jar with shredded tobacco to which I have added a salt/water mixture to get it nice and moist (not sopping wet)
2. Cook for 8 hours at 185°F. I'm not sure why you would want to do a double cook but for dip. It would be a waste of time.
3. Pour hot tobacco into large metal bowl and add glycerin/sweetener.
4. Let cool and age for about a week. (I keep the bowl on a counter top with a lid partially covering the bowl. I fluff up the dip once per day.
5. After about a week or two I will separate the dip into smaller batches and add my various flavorings.

I like Yellow Twist Bud for my dip. It is fairly light in nicotine. I do not use any type of pH altering stuff such as sodium carbonate. Originally dip (snus etc) was made with up to 50% ground up stems. Stems have lower nicotine, so I believe manufacturers started adjusting the pH in their mix to increase the nicotine absorption due to the stems. You do not need sodium carbonate for dip. I think this whole pH adjusting chemical thing began hundreds of years ago.

For a sweetener I use xylitol and pure sucralose. Since I am going to have dip in my mouth I do not want to use sugar. Xylitol has excellent anti-tooth cavity properties as well as anti-microbial properties (the two being related).

The Glycerin benefit is twofold. It has good anti-microbial properties and it adds "mouth feel" to the tobacco. This means that when you put dip in your mouth, all the flavor will not be sucked out in 30 seconds.

The reason I add my flavoring last is because I like a lot of variation in my dip. Sometimes I desire wintergreen, other times black licorice or even orange flavored. I usually make a big batch and, after aging, break it up into smaller batches to store in the freezer. This is completely finished dip with the exception of the flavoring. If I am dipping wintergreen but have the urge for some apple cinnamon I just thaw a baggie of unflavored dip, and add my flavoring.

Dip is easy. Don't over complicate things. As a matter of fact, you don't even need to cook your dip at all. That's just done to kill off any enzymes/bacteria that cause a rise in TSNAs [tobacco specific nitrosamines].

For 1 small batch of dip:
- 3 c packed tobacco
- ½ tsp salt
- 60 cc water

You can double the water if you like. It's an art more than a science
- Add the salt/water solution to the tobacco
- Stir well and let it set for about 20-30 minutes. It will seem very dry at first but after about 20 minutes the tobacco will absorb all of the water.
- Place in a small pint mason jar (the flat squat kind).
- Place jar in a Crockpot.
- Fill completely with water.

You will need to add a weight to the top of the jar otherwise it will float. Make sure your jar is short enough to fit in your Crockpot and completely covered in water.
- Slip in a temperature probe from your Thermostat
- Set for 185°F, and cook for 8 hrs.

I use hot tap water. It'll take about 2 hours to reach 185°F, but that's okay. 8 hours, for the overall process is fine. After 8 hours, use canning tongues (or a thick glove) and remove the jar.
Pour contents into a big bowl.

Add:
- xylitol 2 tsp
- pure sucralose 2 tsp
- glycerin 2 tbsp

Stir with your hands or a fork. Rest, partially covered for 1 to 2 weeks. It'll initially stink. After the waiting period, try some. Then add a flavor of your choice. The amount of flavoring to add is very personal. Start light, and add till you like the taste. I store large amounts in the freezer.

Notes: 2 tbsp glycerin makes a somewhat dry mix, while 4 tbsp makes a wet mix. I like things sweet, so 2 tsp pure sucralose might be too sweet for you. You just need to make small batches to find something you like.

Flavorings I like: wintergreen, anise, orange, maple and apple-cinnamon.

---

tullius (2019): Better Than Grizzly Oral Snus

114 g equal parts by wt. (⅛" shred, all tobaccos WLT) dark air-cured, Tennessee dark fire-cured, misc. Virginia stems
114 g distilled water
18 g coarse (kosher) salt
5 g sodium carbonate (baking soda cooked in oven @ 300°F for 1 hour)

- Bake/dry tobaccos in oven at 275°F for 1 hr
- Pulverize in food processor, sift, pulverize and sift again
- Add salt to water and gently heat until salt dissolves
- Mix salt water solution into pulverized tobacco thoroughly
- Pack mixture tightly into glass canning jars, top with lids, add rings. Cook in water bath at 195°F for 8 hours, rest overnight
- In mixing bowl, dissolve sodium carbonate in 10 g room temp distilled water and add cooked tobacco mixture. Mix well
- Cover tightly with plastic wrap and rest in refrigerator overnight
- Add 25 g of additional distilled water, mix well

- Vacuum seal and store in refrigerator, use as needed

I tried the first rub after 24 hrs on an empty stomach. It was excellent. Made my head spin a little, and I've been chewing Copenhagen and Grizzly since I was 14. Better after 1-2 weeks rest.

The weight of the tobacco flour was calculated after drying, pulverizing and sifting. The added water in the instructions is in addition to the 114 g specified in the ingredient list. Use Morton coarse kosher salt.

COMMENTS:
GreenDragon (2019):
1 teaspoon table salt = 1½ tsp Morton kosher salt = 2 tsp Diamond Crystal kosher salt.

_____

james442 (2015): **Another Take on Squeezyjohn's Oral Snus**

Snus is essentially made from 4 basic ingredients: tobacco, water, salt, alkali

TOBACCO FLOUR
This is simply tobacco leaf that has been ground up to a fine powder. You can buy it from Sweden or make it yourself. The kind of tobacco used in almost every brand of snus today is air-cured or sun-cured. This is because the alternative methods of fire-curing or flue-curing can lead to higher TSNA [tobacco specific nitrosamines] levels, which can in turn increase the risk of mouth cancer. Bearing this in mind, you can create some kind of snus out of every imaginable variety of tobacco if you wish to. The variety or blend used is very influential on the final taste of the snus.

To create flour from your [fully cured and aged] tobacco you will need to first dry it completely. Then you will need to grind it. Coffee grinders with a very fine setting can work, but I do mine in a food blender followed by sieving. Once converted to flour, the tobacco can be kept indefinitely in an airtight [container].

WATER
The only thing to watch out for here is chlorine in tap water, which can develop off tastes in the finished snus. You can use bottled spring water or simply leave a jug of water in the fridge overnight to allow the chlorine to evaporate off naturally.

SALT
Simple salt is an important ingredient in snus, but avoid standard table salt as it may contain iodine and other additives, to make it pour better. Sea salt or Kosher salt are best.

ALKALI
After cooking the snus you need to raise it's pH by adding an alkali to the recipe. This free-bases the nicotine and also develops the characteristic snus taste. Two used are sodium carbonate or potassium carbonate. Potassium carbonate solution can be bought from oriental supermarkets under the name Lye Water. It's food grade and perfect. To make your own sodium carbonate, take some regular baking soda (sodium bicarbonate) and bake it in the oven for at least one hour at *above* the boiling point of water (100°C or 212°F). When it comes out of the oven it is perfect sodium carbonate for making snus with.

FLAVORINGS (OPTIONAL)
There are two ways to flavor your snus. The most common is to add essences or essential oils *after* the cooking process. The other type of flavoring is to add spices such as pepper or cinnamon or sweetening agents such as powdered licorice root. This type of additive is best mixed with the tobacco flour at the beginning.

ADDITIVES (OPTIONAL)
While it is a common aim with home-made stuff to drop the additives in search of a more 'organic' product, several are commonly included in home snus recipes:
  • glycerol (glycerin): this is only for loose snus recipes and holds the snus together for longer

- propylene glycol (PG): a humectant. It keeps the snus from drying out
- salmiak (ammonium chloride): more of a flavoring chemical, popular in Scandinavia. An ammonium salt. It is an acquired taste!

EQUIPMENT
- Heat control: You need to be able to maintain your snus mix at constant high temperatures (up to 85°C or 185°F) for long periods of time (longer than 24 hours). Many different approaches have been tried:
- The Swedish snus oven: basically an insulated cardboard box with an incandescent light-bulb inside it. With a little care and attention, it can maintain a fairly constant temperature, but you need to keep an eye on it.
- A regular oven: a standard kitchen oven can be used to keep temperatures fairly consistent, provided you are not worried about the high energy bills, and no-one else in your house wants to bake for a couple of days. The important thing here is to realize that it's the temperature of the snus that is important, not the temperature the oven is set at. So you need to check with a manual thermometer occasionally, to see how close you are.
- The "*sous-vide*" method: also known as the Crockpot water bath, because commercial *sous-vide* machines are expensive. The much cheaper option is to buy a PID device designed to convert a Crockpot (slow cooker) in to a constant temperature controlled water bath. This method has by far the most control over temperature and needs the least monitoring. [The Crockpot must have an analog (dial) switch, rather than a digital switch. The latter will not automatically switch back on after its power source has been switched off by a PID.]

Other useful items:

- water-tight glass storage jars for the snus (use with the Crockpot)
- weighing scales
- measuring jug
- mixing bowl
- fork
- coffee grinder
- food processor
- fridge

THE BASIC METHOD
- Add the water and salt to the tobacco flour and mix thoroughly. Firstly I dissolve the salt in the water, and then I mix with the tobacco. I find that doing this in a large mixing bowl with a fork is the best way to ensure the water and tobacco are thoroughly mixed together to form a light brown paste. Transfer back to the glass jar and compress down before the next step. A general rule of thumb is using between 100 and 150 ml water and 6-9 g salt per 100 g of tobacco flour. The amount of water depends on how absorbent your particular tobacco flour is. My standard recipe is 120 ml water and 8 g salt per 100 g of tobacco flour. In imperial measures that works out at just over half a c of water and a level tsp of coarse ground salt per ¼ lb of tobacco flour.
- The first cook: The snus then needs to be brought to a high temperature and maintained there. You can go between 55 and 85°C (130–185°F), but the lower the temperature the longer you need. A rough rule of thumb is that the upper temperature of 85°C (185°F) needs to be maintained for at least 24 hours, whereas with the lower temperature of 55°C (130°F) you need at least 6 days. The temperature does have an effect on the taste of the finished product, with lower temperatures keeping far more of the aroma of the original tobacco intact, and higher temperatures tasting dark and more cooked.

The best test of whether your snus is fully cooked is to note the color. When it hits a dark chocolate brown it is ready for the next step.

- Freebasing the nicotine with an alkali: This step is simply to take the snus from it's heat source and add either sodium carbonate or potassium carbonate, mixing thoroughly, and returning to the heat for a further 8 hours. If using dry powdered carbonate, then 5-10 g per 100 g of tobacco flour can be added. The more carbonate you use the stronger [nicotine] your snus will be, but if the pH is very high then the alkalinity can make it hurt your lips, so use common sense. If using potassium carbonate in the form of lye water, add 1½-3 tsp of the solution. Adding 7 g of powder or 2 tsp of lye water is sufficient for a normal strength snus.

You can try your snus at this point, but be warned, it will taste horrible! The reaction with the alkali causes a lot of ammonia to be given off, and the pH will be far too high for your lip too. It will not be good to use until it has had a further week or weeks of aging, to allow the ammonia to gas off.

- Flavoring: This is where you can let your creativity run wild! In addition to the classic essential oils, you can also add just about anything you can eat, provided it can be mixed with the snus properly. Espresso coffee, booze of any description, spices, minced anchovies. The only rule I follow here is that it must not make the snus too wet to use. The other thing to note is that it is VERY easy to over-flavor your snus at this point, especially with essential oils. A nice subtle taste might be achieved with only ¹⁄₁₀ of a drop of essential oil. So experiment with your oils diluted in a little vodka. Otherwise your project might be ruined.
- Aging: What we're doing here is not really aging. It's allowing the reaction started in step by the alkali to completely finish. In the pursuit of freshness it's best done in the fridge or other cold place, and you need to make sure the ammonia gas can escape from the container your snus is sitting in. Meanwhile all the flavor compounds you have added will mingle with the snus. Let this happen for about a week and then test it.

COMMENTS:
Snusser (2016)
- 150 g Virginia Bright Leaf, dried, ground and sifted into flour.
- 50 g Burley, dried, ground and sifted into flour.
- 16 g Salt
- 135 g Water
- 6 h @ 66°C.
- 20 h @ 85°C.
- Remove from heat.
- 16 g Carbonate solution in 40 g of water.
- 12 h @ 66°C.

I cooked this batch with no lid, and stirred the contents of the jar a few times during the cook, to keep the snus 'breathing'.

Results: Batch 3 has been aging for only a day and smells almost like snus should already. The ammonia smell is almost gone. It hand-makes into a *pris* perfectly with this moisture content.

My next batch, even better used:
- 4 parts burley
- 1 part Virginia Bright Leaf

_____

jojjas (2013): How to make Swedish Oral Snus

[NOTE: this recipe is missing the quantity of tobacco flour in relation to the other ingredients.]

Gear needed:
- hand cranked (old style) meat grinder. Don't use your household electric grinder. It will surely die; mine did.
- oven with a good thermometer
- a good scale
- mixer
- some ovenproof plastic containers with lids

It does not have to be a plastic container, but I use a plastic lunchbox, heat resistance to max 120°C (248°F), but the lid has to be sealed, to keep the moisture inside during "cooking".

You could use any kind of tobacco leaf you want. I prefer burley, cigar varieties and or Virginia. Even stems could be used, but they must be very dry, or it becomes too heavy to grind them. You could even use unfermented leaves only if they are dry.

- Grind tobacco leaf to a fine powder, something between fine sawdust and oatmeal flour.
- Add equal parts tobacco flour with boiling water with approx 50-70 g salt [*per ? quantity tobacco flour*]
- Mix well
- Put it in the container, and press it firmly with the end of a wooden plank or something similar. Put on the lid tightly.
- Set oven to about 90°C (±5°C).
- Place the container in the oven for 24 h
- After 24 h, take out the container and mix the tobacco so there are no lumps.

Next step is a little bit critical. Do this out side. If it is hot direct from the oven, it can irritate your eyes and nose when you mix it together.

- Boil 0.25 l water with 40-70 g of sodium carbonate [*per ? quantity tobacco flour*] and add to the tobacco. (I prefer 45-50 g.) If you want stronger (more nicotine, more strength), use the high dosage.
- Put it in the non-reactive container, and press it hard with the end of a wooden plank or something similar.
- Put on the lid and make sure it's tight.
- Place it in the oven for 12 h @ 90°C.
- After 12 h take out the snus from the oven, and let it cool down.
- Mix it well so there are no lumps.
- Add flavor, and if you want, some substance to keep it moist.
- Store it in refrigerator to keep it moist and fresh.

I use the whole leaf, and even use stems from my pipe-tobacco experiments. I like my snus a little bit more course, and usually flavor it with juniper essence (1-2 tsp to 1 kg snus) to taste like Göteborg's Rapé, or flavor it with bergamot for taste like General-snus

To make my snus making easier, I motorized my meat grinder. A 2 hp electric motor does the trick. 0.5 kg was ground in 10 minutes, with stems and all.

I made a batch of snus last week, 9 lbs or 4.1 kg (made 15.5 lbs or 7 kg a month earlier, all gone) with my newly developed recipe. The standard recipe [as above] but added about ¾ oz or 20 grams of ground deer tongue, flavored with 1 tsp juniper oil, tsp bergamot oil, 8 tsp cocoa and 2 tbsp of Calvados (distilled cider).

COMMENTS:
Hasse SWE (2013):
You can do snuff at lower temp, and then increase the time (original recipe is at 70°C in 5-7 days).

Hasse SWE (2015):
One thing is for sure: Making my own is the best thing I ever did.

POGreen (2014):
I use 100°C+ when I treat mine over a period of 1 whole week. Take the batch out every day to check water content, and stir the flour. Storing the batch for some time will do wonders to your own made snus.

_____

wruk53 (2023): Shirazi/Trabzon2 Oral Snus

Started a new batch of snus on Friday using my homegrown Shirazi and Trabzon 2. The tobaccos were well aged this time. I more or less followed the Squeezyjohn Ettan recipe. The proportions and methods I used are as follows:

- 200 g Shirazi flour
- 200 g Trabzon 2 flour
- 32 g kosher salt
- 2 tsp plain baking cocoa powder
- 24 g sodium carbonate
- 400 g RO (reverse osmosis) water.

I poured the tobacco flour and cocoa powder into a mixing bowl and mixed well. Next, I dissolved the salt into 280 g of the water, poured into the flour and mixed until the flour was evenly moist. At that point, I packed it into three pint-sized Mason jars, put the seals in place, and tightened the lids finger tight. I placed the jars into my Instant Pot [IP] with water up to the level of the top of the snus in the jars. Set the IP to medium warm, which maintains at 181 to 183°F. Cooked it for 24 hours, then unpacked the snus into a mixing bowl and alkalized by mixing well with the sodium carbonate mixed into 120 g of warm water and cooked for another 10 hours. The total amount of water used was equal to the amount of tobacco flour by weight. I let the jars sit out on the counter over night to cool down. In the morning, I scraped it out into a bowl, put the lid on, and put it in the fridge for aging.

When this batch was alkalized, it gave off very strong nose burning, eye watering fumes, so I'm certain it will be high in nicotine. The final weight of this batch is approximately 2 pounds. I have high hopes for this batch. I'll let it rest for a week or two, then try it and give a review.

10 Days later:
I sampled my Trabzon 2/Shirazi Snus, and I'm very pleased with it. It is medium high in nicotine content and has a rich tobacco flavor and scent. There won't be any need to add flavorings. Definitely a keeper recipe. It's been in the fridge for 10 days, and normally keeps on improving for a few more weeks. Then I'll divide it into 3 or 4 oz per zip lock baggie, and freeze for long term storage.

COMMENTS:
deluxestogie (2023)
Thanks for the clearly-written recipe, with documented times, measurements and methods. [The "Trabzon 2", from Northwood Seeds, is a Bright Leaf variety collected near Trabzon, Turkey. It's pedigree is unknown, and may or may not share characteristics with the petiolate, Samsun-like Oriental variety known as Trabzon.]

———————————

loui loui (2023): DIY Snus Kit from Swedsnus

- 1 kg tobacco flour
- 80 g salt (NaCl)
- 75 g Sodium Carbonate
- 60 g propylene glycol
- 60 g glycerol (glycerin)

Yield: 2.5 kg finished snus

Instructions:
- boil 1 l water and 80 g salt.
- throw in five bags of Earl Grey Tea and let it steep 4 minutes.
- When the salt water tea was ready, I put the pot on the cold balcony so it cooled down.
- When the tea was cool I mixed the tobacco flour and the salt water tea, mixing with a wooden paddle and my hands, while wearing vinyl gloves. The mix reminded me of loose soil when finished.
- I filled four 1 l IKEA Korken jars with the mix
- The oven was set at 90°C bottom heating.
- The timer was set at 24 h.
- I took it out from the oven, and let it cool down.
- I made 3 dl strong Earl Grey Tea.
- I let the tea cool down to 45°C.
- I unsealed the jars.
- I removed the lumps and made an even mix.
- I took the 45°C Earl Grey Tea and mixed it with 75 g sodium carbonate. I do it on the balcony because it stinks.
- My tools:
  - wooden paddle
  - hand whip
  - pair of vinyl gloves
  - four IKEA Korken 1 litre jars.
- When the Earl Grey Tea & sodium carbonate mix had cooled down to room temperature I mixed it with the snus.

- First I mixed it quickly with the wooden paddle and second with my hands with gloves on.
- When I was done mixing that, I mixed the snus with 60 g of glycerin and 60 g propylene glycol. Again quickly with the wooden paddle and then by hand.
- When done mixing I filled the jars with the snus.
- I placed the jars in the fridge. I will let them stay there two weeks.

———————

Chew

FmGrowit (2011): Loose Chew

(from the survivalistboards.com)

For Loose leaf chew, I recall Pap had some small wooden kegs. Plastic would probably work too. When we stripped the tobacco off the stalks, he'd choose the leaves and pin them on small nails about an inch down from the top of the keg. Once he decided he had enough tobacco in one keg he'd place a small bowl of cut fruit, usually apple, as we had plenty of those, in the middle and he'd sprinkle some juice on the leaves, place the lid tightly and wait about 3 days before he took the fruit out. He'd sprinkle the leaves with more juice and close it for a week or so.

In a 2 quart old pan, he'd thin out molasses with some whiskey (a cheap whiskey is OK here), and soak a lot of tips and "roughage" tobacco. This was the partial leaves or tips of the plants with very small leaves. This was covered and waited for a week also. If there was a lot of unabsorbed juice he'd add more roughage.

Now as he used his chew, he'd take a large handful of his fruited tobacco and then add in enough of his molasses to make it moist but not wet. This stood for a week or so, closed in a foil pack. Then he'd give us our chew. Normally we'd just mix it all at the same time, as we only used apple for the most part, but if you want a variety, mix them separately.

You can also burn a cinnamon stick in the apple keg to effectively "smoke" the tobacco and it's quite nice. I'm sure there are many other things you can do as well.

When tobacco is "in case" it is lightly sticky and doesn't crumble as you handle it. It should feel like it is damp but not wet. The better your tobacco cases the better your plug and chew will be.

If you start making your chew and the weather turns hot, simply place it in a cool place like a root cellar to hold the case.

_____

Jitterbugdude (2011): Chocolate Chew

Put about 2 oz water into a pot, add 1 tsp cocoa and a sweetener of your choice. I use Neotame. If you use sugar, I would guess that 1 tsp might do. Heat this mixture enough to dissolve the cocoa. Stir constantly because the cocoa is going to want to burn on the bottom of the pan. When hot, add your tobacco (about 1 ounce [~28 g]), give it a quick stir and remove from heat. You can also try playing around with this a little by adding a pinch of salt and/or a few drops of vanilla extract. I tried adding a tad bit of coconut oil once thinking it would improve the mouth texture but it made for a pretty crappy chew. From start to finish this should take about 3 minutes to make. Also, too much cocoa will give a gritty mouth feel... experiment!

_____

Jitterbugdude (2011): Caramel Chew

Same thing.. you will have to tweak the quantities to your liking. I put a few ounces of DaVinci (sugar free) caramel syrup in a pot, add some non sugar sweetener, heat, add tobacco, chew. Total prep time is about 2 minutes. I use Neotame (pure) or sometimes sucralose (pure) because I do not want to have sugar next to my teeth, rotting them.

The cultivar of tobacco you use will also make a big difference. Yellow Orinoco is really good for chew. I've tried Burley, Virginia Gold and a Havana. Each tastes different. You will also want to make 3, 4, 5 batches varying the ingredients till you find a combo you like. I like my chew very sweet. My chocolate chew tastes almost like a Hershey bar.

The amount of liquid is tricky. Too much and your chew will be sopping wet. Not enough and it won't evenly soak up the flavors.

The DaVinci Butter Rum flavor is fantastic too!.. I get mine from Netrition

---

hogateb (2011): Caramel Chew

- 20 g burley
- 3 tbsp caramel syrup (not sugar-free)
- 1 tsp sugar
- ⅛ tsp baking soda

1. Heated non tobacco ingredients until boiling
2. Added Tobacco and cooked for 3-4 minutes

Outcome was very sweet & gritty, due to baking soda I think. I will re-try without extra sugar. Big nicotine hit, I think due to baking soda, or could be the variety used too.

---

hogateb (2011): Chocolate Chew

- 30 g burley
- 2 oz water
- 1 tsp cocoa powder
- 2 tbsp sugar
- ⅛ tsp salt
- 2 drops of Vanilla

1. Cooked non tobacco ingredients until boiling and somewhat syrup consistency
2. Added burley and cooked for 4 minutes

Came out gritty and not too sweet. Not my favorite. Try with more sugar.

---

hogateb (2011): **Pepsi Chew**

- 25 g burley
- 1 can Pepsi
- 1 tbsp sugar

1. Cooked non tobacco ingredients until syrup consistency
2. Add burley stir and cook for 4-5 minutes

Came out okay. Not too sweet. My favorite so far.

Jitterbugdude (2013): **Chew**

I make chew all the time. I do not make much of a distinction between dip and chew, although most people do. You do not need sugar type sweeteners, nor should you want to use sugar type sweeteners. They just contribute to tooth decay. I use pure Neotame and/or pure sucralose for my sweetener. It amazes me how complicated people make things. Just take a handful of shredded leaf, add your sweetener of choice, some concentrated flavoring (from LorAnn Oils) and enough liquid to get it to the consistency you want. That should take you about 3 minutes, and you are done. I like to add a little bit of glycerin to my mix. Once you've made a "baseline" batch you can then start changing the proportions around to suit your needs. For starters, here's a recipe I use that I like:

- 1 oz (~28 g) shredded leaf (I like Yellow Orinoco the best, but Yellow Twist Bud is good too)
- 1 tbsp xylitol. This is a sugar free sweetener that actually prevents tooth decay. It is not needed though, because it does not add much sweetness to the mix. I only include it for its anti-cavity ability.
- ⅛ tsp pure sucralose. You will have to play around with this, since some people like their dip/chew sweeter than others.
- 1 tbsp glycerin. It improves the mouth-feel of the chew/dip
- 1 tsp pure wintergreen oil
- 40 cc water. This is approximate. Add enough to make it as wet as you want. 40 cc will give you a fairly wet product.

1. Mix everything together in a bowl.
2. Stir it up a few times a day, to let the contents absorb into the leaf.
3. If it st too wet to your liking, just spread it out on the table and in a day or two it will be dry.

You can also try warming this up in a pot for a few minutes to help dissolve everything better but I find that is not necessary.

By using wintergreen or cinnamon oil, this will never mold. But be aware that if you are using other sweeteners, such as apple, it will mold within a few days.

I've tried air-cured flue varieties, burley, Oriental and Maryland. The oriental tasted odd as a chew.

RyanM22 (2014): Simple Loose Leaf Chew

Ingredients:
- whole tobacco (5-7 leaves). I used BigBonner's dark air-cured.
- fruit juice of choice (100% juice works best)
- molasses 1 tbsp
- glycerin 1 tbsp
- salt to taste

Prepping the leaf:
1. Lay out some paper towels, and spray the dry leaf with some water on both sides. Get it good and wet and let them sit out and absorb the water. Takes about an hour.
2. Once wet, strip lamina from the midrib
3. Roll up the leaves and use scissors to cut into strips. I like thin strips about 1½ inches long.
4. Toss strips into a plastic bag, and spray with a little more water. Shake up the bag to make sure all the leaf is wet.

Making the sauce:
1. Boil 100% juice. Enough to fill the bottom of an average pan is plenty. After it's bubbling for about a minute, turn the heat down to medium. You want to make it into syrup. In total this takes less than 10 minutes. Keep an eye on it because on high

temps it'll burn easily (learned that the hard way). With 100% juice there's no need to drain off water.

2. Once it starts to get thick, turn the heat off and add 1 tbsp molasses. I use Wholesome Sweetener's Organic. Mix it up with a wooden spoon.
3. Add leaf and keep mixing. Make sure the heat's off at this point, but keep it on the burner to keep everything warm.
4. Add 1 tbsp glycerin, and mix in.
5. Add a healthy amount of salt [??] (sea salt works best)
6. Mix until all the syrup is soaked up, and leave it on the burner for 1-2 hours tops.

Finish:
Transfer to plastic bag and let it sit for a week, so all the flavor is absorbed.

For the juice, I've used a mix of 75% prune and 25% grape for a Redman-like flavor, and pure apple. Cherry is next. Tried the apple because I'm impatient and while it packs a damn good punch, you're better off letting it sit for a week

Once you find a flavor you like, make the syrup beforehand. Boiling small amounts of juice burns easily. Boil off a lot of juice (however much you can fit in a pan), and once it gets thick take it off the burner, let it cool and put it in the fridge. It'll thicken even more, and you can take as much as you like and warm it up slightly with the rest of the ingredients.

Michibacy (2012): **Apple Chew**
- De-stem/shred tobacco
- Heat up 3 c apple juice (basic apple juice)
- Boil down to ~ 2 c in the pan
- Mix in another 1 cup juice
- Boil down so there is 2 c of juice in the pan
- Add 4 heaping tbsp molasses
- Stir those ingredients altogether so that it's homogeneous
- Remove from heat

- Add leaf and mix
- Soak the leaves in the brine for a few days in a Ziploc bag. This really reduces the harshness of the tobacco if there is any.
- Set it out to dry on a cookie sheet (stay away from dust etc that could contaminate the tobacco)
- Let it air dry, if possible with a small fan to help the tobacco dry

Jitterbugdude (2012): Chew

Yellow Twist Bud and Yellow Orinoco are my favorites for chew, but air-cured Perique (variety) and most any burley works good too.

You don't have to jump through all those hoops to make chew.

- Grab a handful of shredded tobacco, add:
- 1 tbsp water
- 1 tbsp (or more) sugar
- a flavoring of your choice

Flavoring could be mint, apple extract, cocoa etc. If using an extract, add ½ tsp, if adding cocoa add 1 tbsp.

1. Put everything together in a pan and heat for about 1 minute.
2. You are now done.

You also now have a known product to work with. The next time you might find you'll want to add more sugar or less, more flavoring or less, etc. If your chew is too moist just let it set out overnight, or cook for a minute more, stirring constantly.

Hasse SWE (2013): Chew #1

- 100g tobacco (*Nicotiana tabacum*)
- 2 dl (~7 oz) Apple juice
- 2-4 pinches of salt
- cornstarch (to taste)
- ⅓ dl sugar (~2¼ tbsp)

Start by adding the tobacco to a bowl, add apple juice until all tobacco is moistened. There should absolutely not be any dry leaves or crumbs. Should something be dry, add a little more juice.

Roll the tobacco in foil.

Add the tobacco "sausage" to a baking tray, and place it in the oven at 80°C. Bake 24 to 36 h.

Once the tobacco has baked 24-36 hours, unroll the tobacco out of the foil, and sprinkle ⅓ dl (~2¼ tbsp) sugar and the cornstarch in a little tobacco. Roll the tobacco in foil again, and bake it in the oven 30-60 minutes until the sugar and starch dissolve into tobacco.

Allow the tobacco to cool and mature a few days in the refrigerator, so that the flavor will be better.

Hasse SWE (2013): Chew #2

Pour apple juice (100% natural) in a frying pan. Let it mostly boil away. Pour more. Repeat this three or four times, until the apple juice has been given a golden brown character. Then add ⅓ cup syrup. Stir and add one or two pinches of salt. Stir again. Now you take the pan off the heat and pour in the crushed tobacco and stir. (I used three large cigars that I smashed, in the absence of other tobacco) Allow it to soak up the apple juice and syrup. Now everything should be dark in color and feel sticky. Let everything dry a little bit, so that tobacco has a chewy and slightly sticky feel. It should not be too wet. Take a pinch between your fingers. If you can you make a ball of it, it's the right consistency.

Michibacy (2014): Chaw

- 6 Yellow Twist Bud leaves, stemmed and shredded

Base flavor:
- 1 oz molasses
- 1 tbsp water
- 1 pinch of salt

(mixed to a slurry)

Top flavor:
- 5 drops peppermint oil (not extract)
- 1 tbsp vodka/gin

- 1 tbsp water

Once mixed, the liquid may turn slightly yellow.

Steps:

1. Apply base flavor to the tobacco
2. Let it soak up the proper amount of fluid. Don't just dump it all in.
3. Apply top flavor
4. Mix well
5. Soak for 3 hours
6. Aerate for 12 hours
7. Place in a container

Enjoy after a few hours of soaking and drying.

The molasses turns into what I have officially begun to call the "base flavor". It is on the low end of flavors that you don't really notice in tobacco. For a "high end" or top flavor I use mint oils (food grade), and dilute them with a bit of alcohol and water, then apply to the shredded tobacco. It will make a strong smelling soggy mess. I let that soak for about 3 hours, then begin to aerate the container of tobacco, It begins to clump and fluff. After 12 hours it has dried enough. I deposit it into a used chew can. The right amount of moisture for me is enough to be noticeably moist, but when squeezed it doesn't ring out any fluid.

This makes a really nice peppermint chew. Not too fine cut, and actually tastes like mint, not shredded cardboard with toothpaste.

COMMENTS:

Jitterbugdude: When making chewing tobacco you really should use a non caloric sweetener. Why keep a wad of sugar laden tobacco in your mouth all day? It may taste good now but you'll feel the pain later at the dentist's office. There are several places that sell pure, non caloric sweeteners. You want the pure product because the stuff you buy in the grocery store (in little packets) is mostly maltodextrin which not only tastes "odd" but will raise blood sugar levels just as regular sugar does.

ArizonaDave (2012): Cigar Oval Cuts

Acacia fiber, is sold at health food stores (also known as gum Arabic). I mix in a small amount of water, not much, a few drops will do, to get the paste thick. Then I add nutmeg, cinnamon, and stevia liquid into the paste. I'll take a cigar I rolled and cut it into circular cuts, lay them out on wax paper, put the glue on top of each circle, then let it dry for 2 hours. Excellent flavor!

Jitterbugdude (2015): Spitless Chew

Just cut down the amount of salt, and don't add potassium carbonate because it changes the pH, which will make you spit.

---

squeezyjohn (2015): Sugar-free Chew

I make a sugar free twist by this method. It's a northern European salted chew, but if you don't want it you can leave the salt out.

I take a 4 inch liquorice root, and hammer it in to fragments, then place in a saucepan with a little water (about 200 ml) and 1 tsp salt. I boil it down until the liquid has reduced by half and then strain and cool the liquid. The liquorice doesn't have a lot of flavour but it adds a natural tooth-friendly sweetness. I then take that cooled liquid, add one teaspoon of propylene glycol (stops it from drying out too much) and a few drops of bergamot essential oil as a nice flavouring. You could use any flavouring if you like as long as it's food-safe.

I then brush this mixture on the de-stemmed tobacco leaf and when pliable enough, I roll it up into twists, and hang the twists to dry.

[see image, page 72]

With all these kinds of recipes, there's a bit of trial and error needed. You could use a booze of your choice, substitute the liquorice for xylitol, even add brewed coffee as a flavouring. I find that without sugar, the propylene glycol is pretty essential, as it dries up rock hard otherwise.

ArizonaDave (2016): Tubular chew

I started using a type of tobacco product I make that closely resembles tiny cigars as chew sticks made out of cigar ligero. [Apply cigar glue to the entire outer margin, when rolling.] They average around 7" long, but the ring is closer to a 32 (½ inch diameter). They're infused with a rum vanilla mixture, then I let them air out a bit, to let the alcohol out. They sit in cedar for a few days, after which I cut them into 1" or longer sections. Basically they're self contained, pretty concealed, and can be used anywhere. Most people have no clue I have tobacco in my mouth.

---

squeezyjohn (2016): Propylene glycol for chew

I've found that with chew, you only need a really small amount of propylene glycol in the mix to keep the twists from drying out. About ½ tsp for a litre of casing mix does it fine. Probably less would also work. The thing to bear in mind when applying casing to a twist is that ALL of the water component will evaporate away as they dry, so the flavours/effects really concentrate down from how they are when you taste them in solution.

---

squeezyjohn (2015): *rustica* twist chew

The variety of *Nicotiana rustica* that has been the most successful [for me] is *N. rustica* (Mahorka Stalingradskaia). This variety is of good strength and has large leaves ideal for making twists from. It also has thinner, less rubbery leaves than most *rusticas*, which makes for a better texture in the mouth. It also has a nice mild tobacco flavour, without needing a lot of aging.

The leaves are simply air-cured until brown. I found that with all *rusticas*, a week or so of pile curing (stacking the leaves and leaving to sweat, with re-stacking every few days to prevent decomposition) helped massively in getting them to cure brown rather than slightly green.

Once cured, I take the stems out, and prepare to start twisting. [This recipe uses de-stemmed leaf halves.]

First I make a sauce, to get the snus flavour in to the tobacco:
- approx 500 ml spring water
- 8 crushed liquorice roots
- 50 crushed allspice berries
- 5 tsp sea salt
- 4 tsp salmiak (food-grade ammonium chloride)

The liquorice roots and allspice berries were added to the water in a saucepan, brought to a boil, then simmered until the mixture was dark brown and slightly reduced to 400 ml. It was sieved, and then the salt and salmiak were dissolved in it. This was left to cool down. The liquorice is important, as it adds a sweetness which will not damage your teeth in the way that sugar would. The allspice berries were for a slightly spicy aroma, but other flavouring herbs and spices could be used.

The twist is then formed by laying out about 4 medium sized, de-stemmed leaf halves in a row, overlapping half-way to the next leaf with the straight edge facing you. The leaves are then sprayed lightly with the sauce mixture using a plant-sprayer. The twist is formed by starting at the left hand side and rolling at 45° to the straight edge away from you and towards the right. Keeping the twist as tightly rolled as you can, this feels like rolling a really strange, tight cigar. You can choose a nice big leaf to use as a wrapper for the whole thing if you want it to look neat, or you can just have it as it is. The aim is to make a twist with a diameter of about ⅜", and certainly no wider than ½". At the end, continue to twist both ends in opposite directions so that it starts to loop around itself to form a miniature classic twist shape.

Finish off with a piece of wire or string to hold it together. The final stage is to spray the outside with the sauce again and hang the twists up to dry. The finished twists will be approximately 4" long when doubled up.

To use, simply cut off a small piece (about ¼" long is great for me) and place in your upper lip with the cross-section part touching your gums. As soon as it begins to rehydrate, you get a great, satisfying hit in just the way you do with snus, with all the salty-sweet flavours, along with a nice smooth tobacco taste.

One of these little twists will give you about 35 pieces. They last for hours, and can be refreshed easily by giving them a little bite (but not a full on chew otherwise they can disintegrate). When you dispose of them, they are in one piece rather than having a mouth full of mud. They cause almost no brown colour of the saliva and need no spitting, provided you don't keep messing with them. As soon as they are dry they can be stored somewhere at room temperature and regular humidity in a box or similar. If you want to add extra flavours to them then they can be stored in a sealed jar with aromatic things such as coffee beans, vanilla pods or spices and they will absorb the aroma.

From swedishmatch.com: Chewing Tobacco
Ingredients
Products:
- Red Man (RM)
- Red Man Golden Blend (RMGB)
- Red Man Silver Blend (RMSB)
- Red Man Select (RMS)
- Granger Select (GS)
- Work Horse (WH)
- Brown Mule's Plug (BMP)
- Natural Leaf Plug (NLP)
- Red Man Plug (RMP)
- Tinsley Plug (TP)

All Reviewed Products (Unless Noted):
- **Tobacco**: 23.9-35.4% (note: "plug" varieties had both a higher tobacco % and lower water % limit)

- **Water** (noted as "processing aid and solvent" on RMP): 21.0-29.2%
- **Sucrose** ("flavour"-- common table sugar): 13.9-22.4% (not included in RMSB)
- **Corn Syrup** ("flavour"): 10.5-14.7% (all but RMSB and BMP)
- **Sodium Chloride** ("taste enhancer"): 0.3-2.2%
- **Licorice** ("flavour"): 1.1-6.8% (6.8% as outlier; next highest is 1.9%)
- **Glycerol** ("humectant"-- for retaining moisture): 0.3-3.5%
- **Propylene Glycol** ("humectant"): 0.6-2.2% (highest in chew, lowest in plug)
- **Natural and Artificial Flavours**: 0.7-1.8% for chew, 0.1% for all plug except RMP @ 1.7%
- **Sodium Saccharine** ("sweetener"): 0.1-0.2%
- **Sodium Benzoate** ("preservative"): 0.1%
- **Potassium Sorbate** ("preservative"): 0.1-0.3% (not included in BMP)

Mollasses (flavour):
Included in RM, RMGB, RMS, GS, WH, RMP at 5.5-6.4%

Sodium Bicarbonate ("acidity regulator"):
Included in RM, RMSB, WH, RMP at 0.1%

Invert sugar ("flavour"):
Included in RMGB, RMS, GS, NLP, TP at 2.3-7.6% (higher in plug)

Food starch (thickener):
Inlcluded in RMGB, RMS at 0.1-0.2%

Caramel ("humectant/flavour"):
Included in Granger Select at 0.1%

Plug wrap light:
Included in NLP, TP, RMP 1.8-3.2%, noted at 2.6% and wrap "dark," not "light," for BMP

Sorbitol ("humectant"):
Included in RMP at 2.3% and BMP at 6.8%

Acacia (gum arabic) ("emulsifier"):
Included in NLP and TP at 2.1%

Benzoic Acid ("preservative"):
Included in Brown Mule's Plug at 0.1%

_____

Michibacy (2013): "Licorice" Twist
- ¼ cup honey
- ¼ cup water
- 2½ tsp anise extract
- 10 ounces of dry tobacco. I broke it up into large flakes. I used Yellow Twist Bud and some Virginia Bright Leaf (VBL).
  NOTE: Don't use VBL, it doesn't darken like classic chew.

1. Heat water and honey in a pan until it's a soupy fluid.
2. Add 1½ tsp anise extract (If using anise oil use ½ tsp)
3. Mix in tobacco and stir
4. Heat over low stove temp until there is no remnant liquid remaining in the pan. Tilt the pan sideways a bit and hold/press the moistened tobacco to make any seep out to check if it's dry enough.
5. Put onto a cookie sheet.
6. Drip 1 more tsp anise extract (or ¼ tsp anise oil) over tobacco.
7. Place in 300°F oven for 15 minutes to begin drying tobacco.
8. Remove, and allow to air dry for 24 hours.
9. Make into bricks, plugs or use as loose leaf.

This has a very strong black licorice and root beer flavor, with a very subtle taste of sweetness, but not specifically honey.

_____

nunapitchuk (2019): Dark Air-Cured Dip / Chew

By weight, I use a $30 digital scale that I bought on Amazon. I do 3 batches (pint jars) at a time, because they fit in my boiling pot.

- 200 g dark air-cured leaf, stemmed
- 10 g of glycerin
- 35 g of salt
- 190 g of hot strong brewed dark roast coffee
- pint Mason jar(s)

1. Grind up tobacco in food processor to about the consistency of traditional store-bought rough cut chew or dip.
2. Leave the ground leaves in the food processor.
3. Put **pint jar** on scale, zero, and add 10 g of glycerin to the jar.
4. Zero the scale and add 35 g of salt to the jar.
5. Zero again and add 190 g of hot strong brewed dark roast coffee to the jar.
6. Put lid on the jar and shake to dissolve all the salt.
7. Turn food processor on and add the coffee, salt and glycerin mixture to the running food processor.
8. When it is completely mixed, pack it all into the pint jar. It will just fill the jar if packed in tight.
9. Seal the jar.
10. Put it in warm water bath as deep as possible without floating jar(s).
11. Cover and bring to boil, then turn heat down to low, and let it boil slowly for 5 hours.
12. Remove from water bath, let cool overnight.
13. Store in fridge.

I like this recipe. I would choose this over the store bought stuff that I have been using for years. One packed, pint jar is roughly equivalent to 13 cans of store bought dip (1.2 oz cans).

———————

Rednekf350 (2021): **Burley Chew**

I cooked down store-bought apple juice to a syrup consistency, added two healthy tablespoons of molasses and added a little Kosher salt. The liquid smelled awesome. I broke up half of a large soup pot of de-stemmed Burley leaves and kept folding it in. Folding to coat everything got a little muddy so I added a little more tobacco until I got a better consistency. It is still ridiculously tacky.

I used a quart of apple juice cooked down to an unknown but far smaller quantity, and two heavy tablespoons of molasses. I would guess it was at least 4 oz of reduced apple juice. It was enough to saturate half of a 10 quart soup pot of de-stemmed, dried burley leaves.

After a cool down, I balled up a wad and tried it. I am very happy with the outcome. It has a good, mild tobacco flavor and It has a tang from the apple and sweetness from the reduced apple juice and the molasses. Within 5 minutes I could feel the nicotine but the tobacco didn't burn the mouth.

I am going to put it into a mason jar and store it in the refrigerator for now.

I had another pull out of the jar 2 days later, and it tastes so good it actually makes me want to eat it! The nicotine is very noticeable, but the flavor is sweet and mellow. The finished texture right now is a like a sticky wad of coarse ground oats. I had to pry some out of the with a fork. I'm thinking of adding some glycerin in the next batch and reducing the molasses a little.

COMMENTS:
Jbg (2021):
I did learn that for chewing tobacco, you want a VERY thin syrup, basically slightly thickened juice.

———————————

Rednekf350 (2022): **Little Yellow Chew**

A batch of Little Yellow loose-leaf chew with 2021 homegrown tobacco. I am pleased with the outcome. It doesn't have the grassiness that the batch I made in the fall had.

I cooked down a full quart of apple juice in a 12" stainless pan until it became a light syrup. Noticeably sweeter and slow to roll across the pan. I then added 4 overflowing tablespoons of dark molasses and stirred it in. I added the tobacco which I had already de-stemmed after air curing at the end of last summer. I kept folding in the tobacco with a spatula until all the liquid was absorbed by the tobacco. It was still a little wet looking. I added about 2 oz of Jim Beam Black over the pile, and mixed that in. I put the whole pile in a strainer and pressed it until I got most of the liquid out. I then put it back in the pan at a low heat for about ten minutes, trying to dry it a little more. I didn't want to cook it so I put it back in the strainer for an hour and called it quits. I will keep it in the freezer in Mason jars.

The flavor is good, and no grassy flavor. The nicotine content seems pretty high and you can feel a little jolt after a few minutes.

COMMENTS:
Jbg (2022)
Sodium carbonate raises the ph, making it less hospitable to bacteria and mold, and freebases the nicotine, making it more available for the body to absorb.

Salt improves flavor and helps shelf life some.

Propylene glycol is a humectant(retains moisture), has some anti-fungal properties, and helps your flavor last longer.

Glycerin is another humectant, and is sweet, but it is odd flavored, and mildly antibacterial. It helps with flavor too.

———————————

plantdude (2022): Close to Grizzly Long Cut Wintergreen Chew

- dried tobacco 80-120 g
- water 7 tbsp
- salt 2½ – 3½ tsp
- molasses 1-2 tbsp
- honey 2 tsp
- whiskey 2-3 tbsp
- sodium carbonate 1½–3½ tsp fine powder
- glycerin 1½ tbsp
- propylene glycol ¾ tsp

For tobacco I use anything and everything that is not moldy and not cigar quality. Suckers, green leaf, not aged enough... It does decrease quality, but cook it hotter and longer and add more flavoring and it's okay. Use good quality aged tobacco and it's better. This recipe is not a recipe for purists that just want to cook a few specific types of tobacco and enjoy the distinct flavor of each variety. Instead it's a recipe that can be used to cook many different types of tobacco, add flavor, and approach something that can be bought commercially, while being made somewhat consistently in taste, despite the variety being used. Read that as the nicotine hit is there and the flavor is at the cook's discretion.

I start with low case tobacco, roll it like a cigar, chop it fine with a knife then throw in a coffee grinder to get the desired cut I want. Very low case tobacco breaks apart as you attempt to roll it and requires even less cutting and grinding. After I get a little under a half gallon Ziploc bag full, I use the following recipe. You'll want to adjust for case and personal preference as needed.

Dried tobacco 80-120 g (a little under ½ gallon Ziploc bag of fine shredded dried tobacco) added to a large bowl. Case influences weight a great deal, so it takes a little experimenting.

In a measuring cup:

Add water (Add more as needed to make desired moistness.)

1. Heat water and stir in salt, molasses and honey, to dissolve.
2. Add to tobacco and mix in large bowl. Give tobacco time to re-hydrate.
3. Add whiskey for flavor and to clean out measuring cup and add to tobacco. You may need to add more water (5 -10 tbsp slowly while stirring) depending on case. You want to get it to desired moisture at this stage. Whiskey is more forgiving than water if you are worried about making it too wet.
4. Pack firmly into ¼ pint Mason jars. A little under ½ gallon Ziploc of dried tobacco will be about 5 firmly packed ¼ pint mason jars.
5. Put lids on tightly, loosen slightly about ¼ turn. Add water in (cool) Crockpot to tobacco level. (I add a few small stones on the lids to keep the jars from moving around if the temp gets too high)
6. Cook 24-48 hours on low. Cook crappy, un-aged, green tobacco closer to 48 hours at higher temp. Good tobacco works at 24 hours on low setting.
7. Take jars of tobacco out of Crockpot and let them cool enough to handle.
8. Pour tobacco from jars into large mixing bowl. Save your jars to repack the tobacco in latter.
9. Add sodium carbonate, and stir in. (Use less sodium carbonate if using rustica or high nicotine content tobacco.) Sodium carbonate can burn your mouth at higher concentrations. It acts as an alkali to increases nicotine absorption, so use your best judgment, and use with caution. Make sure it is a fine powder with no chunks, add slowly and mix well.

In a mixing cup add:
*   whiskey 1-2 tbsp
*   glycerin makes it stay moist but can impart a gummy texture and funny flavor if too much used.
*   propylene glycol (omit if desired). It's mainly a preservative to keep mold at bay, and moisturizer.

- Flavoring: 3½ tsp (increase if needed – I prefer more) (LorAnn superstrength wintergreen flavoring. The choice is yours).
- Add slowly to tobacco while stirring, and mix well.
- Add additional whiskey to clean flavoring and glycerin off implements, and add to tobacco.
- Add water (or whiskey) very sparingly while stirring to bring to desired moistness if needed. (Better to over moisten slightly, as you can dry down latter if needed).
- Re-pack firmly into ¼ pint jars.
- Remove jar lid and replace with cheese cloth or paper towel.
- Let sit for a few days at room temp or in the fridge before use. Don't rush this step, you are chemically altering at this stage, and it allows the ammonia produced by the sodium carbonate to tone down a bit, and the excess carbonate to revert to sodium bicarbonate (baking soda).
- Shake occasionally.

Nasal Snuff

SmokesAhoy (2015): Nasal Snuff

- Dark Air-cured 70%
- Light Fire-cured 30%

Dry out 3 of the massive fire-cured leaves and a half pound of dark air-cured. Blend it up into powder. Sift it.

- ground and sieved tobacco flour ¼ cup
- distilled water 2 tsp
- calcium hydroxide (washing soda) ⅛ tsp
- table salt ½ tsp

Dissolve soda and salt in water then add to tobacco flour.
Jar and let sit for one week.

Basically you just mix it. I mix the ingredients and then pour over the sifted tobacco in a Ziploc bag, massage it and mix it well. I take one of the [poly-nylon] tobacco bags I get from wholeleaftobacco.com, and cut it the same size as the baggie and seal it with my wife's hair iron to age. I do about 2 cup batches, since without the heating process of snus, it takes longer to age and mature.

CobGuy (2016): The Most Basic Nasal Snuff

Making your own snuff can be as simple, or complex, as you want to make it. The MOST basic snuff is literally whole-leaf tobacco ground into a flour, with no additional processing or additives. It's strength and character are entirely dependent on the tobacco variety or blend of varieties used.

In decreasing order of nicotine absorption (a wild average) from the nasal cavity:
- *N. rustica*
- Perique (pressure-cured)
- Dark (air-cured or fire-cured) varieties
- Cigar varieties (ligero downward to seco)
- Burley (tips downward to lugs)
- Maryland (tips downward to lugs)
- Flue-cured Virginia Red (upper leaves)
- Flue-cured Virginia Lemon (lower leaves)
- Latakia
- Sun-cured Samsun-type Orientals (Samsun, Bafra, Trabzon, Katerini, etc.)
- Sun-cured Basma-type Orientals (Basma, Xanthi, Izmir, Krumovgrad, etc.)

Huffelpuff (2016): Coconut Mocha Menthol Nasal Snuff
- 30 g tobacco flour
- 5-10 g Coconut Mocha coffee
- 2½-5 g of hot chocolate mix (cocoa powder and sugar)
- Menthol crystals to taste. I use less than ½ gram for this quantity.
- Salt to taste usually between 1-3 grams is all you'll need

Grind all together until super fine, and sift.

You can alkalize the tobacco flour *prior to adding flavorants*, by adding sodium carbonate at a rate of 1-3 g per 100 g of tobacco flour. You'll need to add distilled water to make a paste from the tobacco, sodium carbonate and salt. Let it sit in a warm spot covered for a week or two, then dry it out, and regrind it. Then you can mix in coffee, chocolate and menthol if desired. Eucalyptus is a nice addition to nasal snuff. I use essential oil for that.

smokesahoy (2017): Make nasal snuff from wet snus

Make snus. Let it age per directions. After a couple weeks, dehydrate it, and give it a real good grind again, sieving to desired mesh. I added a drop of bergamot too, during the grinding sieving stage. It's usable immediately and fantastic. It's funny that snus was originally snuff processed for wet oral use, but it makes an intense snuff if dried back out and ground super fine. I find it nicer than the uncooked version.

---

wooda2008 (2017): *N. rustica* Nasal Snuff raw—68 Olson

68 Olson, *Nicotiana rustica*
ARS-GRIN:
TR 18
PI 499176

Leaf fragments broke off while I was boxing them. I ground up with a few grains of salt in the Magic Bullet coffee grinder, and toasted at 250°F for 20 minutes.

Very delicate floral flavor, gently transitioning to toasted cocoa. Initial intense head pressure, and racing pulse. Post nasal drip is less harsh than Chef Daniel's Acadia snuff. Ten minutes in with no additional bump, the nicotine hit is not abating in the slightest. Rather, it is building. Not bad for 12 days post harvest. Stayed up all night staring at the ceiling. Took another dose early this morning. Better than coffee. I left this open to the air all week, and took another toot this morning before my commute. It has mellowed more.

Take 2: All yellow or yellow-brown leaf from the second batch of pile-cured 68 Olson, ground fine. It's awesome. Smells like fresh hay and clean cow. Brings me back to playing in the hay loft at my cousin's beef farm as a little kid. I feel the hit in my front teeth and the base of my skull. Very little throat burn on post nasal drip with the yellow cured. Fantastic "toot."

CobGuy (2020): One Sucker Nasal Snuff

One Sucker as the base flour, I added 2.2 g CaOH (calcium hydroxide, lime) in 100 g water to 220 g tobacco flour.

The grind is coarse and the snuff is moist. Initial trial is reminiscent of Taxi Red or NTSU Black.

I've named this one "Sucker Punch". No cooking this time. Just the few simple ingredients listed above. I use a food processor and a series of sieves to end at 600 micron for the final product. This has really become my "go to" style of snuff—natural and strong.

CobGuy (2020): Nasal Snuff

I use whole leaf from wholeleaftobacco.com, burley and cigar varieties mostly, but have made a few using flue-cured too.

How to prepare it: Food processor, coffee grinder, mortar and pestle, various sizes of sieves (EZ-Strainer fits 5 gallon buckets). Initial grinding and sauce making in a day. Several weeks to months sitting / fermenting time. [EZ-Strainer sieves available at www.usplastic.com]

I either make my own sauces and reductions, or buy food grade extracts. If I can't eat it I don't use it. Here's an example:
- 2 c double-fermented soy sauce
- 2 heaping tbsp dark molasses
- 1 tsp black walnut extract
- fennel seeds
- dark roasted coffee

1. Heat the mixture to a simmer and continue slowly until it thickens slightly.
2. Pour the sauce through the finely ground coffee and strain.
3. Apply this to shredded leaf, enough to completely wet it, but not dripping wet.
4. Place the mix into a press for 3-5 days. I use a 6 ton shop press.
5. Remove from the press.
6. Dry it enough for first milling.

7. Jar for at least 3 weeks.
8. Grind and sieve to desired micron (400μ for a coarse and moist blend, 200μ for fine and dry).
9. Either toast or re-hydrate, and back into jars.

I called it "Savory", kind of an Umami that fades to chocolaty.

As simple or complex as you want to make it.
Grind up some Burley into flour and add Vanilla extract, and you're done!

I bought the 600, 400 and 200 micron sizes of sieves, and find them to work well. The 400 is my minimum "finished" size.

New flavored oils:
- Wintergreen (smells like original Life Savers)
- Apple (not what I expected but a nice fruity scent)
- Bubblegum (spot on for Bazooka!)
- Coffee (more like a Kahlua scent)
- Orange-Vanilla (memories of childhood Creamsicles!)
- Bubblegum with a drop of Wintergreen = Pepto Bismol

These will be fun to play with and make some faster, easier snuffs that don't require as much fermentation time.

COMMENTS:
Ifyougotem (2020):
Prilep: It's fantastic, raw & straight out of the bag, with outstanding, full floral aroma, and mild nicotine. No harsh aspects whatsoever. I found it easy to pulverize to dust just grinding it together w fingertips, then passed it through a fine wire-mesh strainer (tapping the rim, without scrubbing it through). Decided to bump up the nicotine with some dark air-cured (DAC), processed exactly the same, without a coffee grinder even (though I'd use one if processing in bulk).
- 75% Prilep
- 20-25% DAC

This seems to be the stiffest nicotine blend that seems balanced to me. In my short experience, any more DAC, and the Prilep floral aroma is attenuated adversely. Those wanting it mild could cut back the DAC further, or even enjoy the Prilep straight-up. Lovin' it. No casing, no additives, one common tool, and copious aroma from just the raw leaf itself.

When pulverized to flour in a mortar, it stings quite a bit (and packs a greater and more immediate nicotine punch too, since there's quite a bit more tobacco in a pinch.) As with cigarette shred, the particle size has a major influence on nasal snuff characteristics. I may leave out the extra-fine grinding. I consider the slightly coarser grind to be a sort of "time delay" delivery mechanism. Even the solo Prilep had a noticeable little nip in flour form, but zero when less finely ground.

SmokesAhoy (2017): Nasal Snuff

- flour is a mix of fire-cured and dark air-cured. I like 60:40 or 50:50 personally.
- salt 4% of tobacco weight
- Splenda ½-1% tobacco weight
- cherry oil

I use LorAnn's black cherry. This could be any flavoring or none at all. To get a small enough amount in to the mix I dip a length of wire about the diameter of a small sewing needle in to the oil and rub it back and forth through the powder.

Process into powder in a coffee mill, using air-dried tobacco. Remove. The more stems you use, the milder the nicotine in the end product.

Powder your salt in the empty mill. I use kosher salt, because it seems the easiest to get it into a very fine powder. Mix in the sweetener, and powder more in the mill. Add to tobacco flour back into the mill, and buzz in the mill for another minute. Sieve to size, and continue powdering anything that doesn't sieve.

When everything is powdered, and still in your coffee grinder, add the cherry oil to the mix by swiping the wire back and forth through the flour. Powder will stick to the wire. Scrape it on the grinder blade.

Buzz in the coffee grinder again for another minute or more.

Sieve one last time and put in to an airtight container. It's good right away, but over time the flavors meld, and the cherry begins to come through subtly.

This is fully as good as any American scotch, a smokey snuff where the cherry melds wonderfully with the smoke, and there is just enough salt and sweetener to make it taste very good, without being either salty or sweet. Cherry doesn't come through as cherry, since not enough was used. But it modifies the fire cured to have a different character: softer and sweeter. If you're also a fan of American scotch, give this a try.

RattlerViper (2021): **Alkakizer for Nasal Snuff**
Making sodium carbonate. I took baking soda, and spread it on a cookie sheet, then baked it at 400°F for an hour, to turn the sodium bicarbonate into sodium carbonate.

I used the sodium carbonate 9 g to 100 g of tobacco flour. It has a very healthy nicotine kick. Adjust your volume of alkalizer to suit your needs.

Levi Gross (2022): **Easy Nasal Snuff Dispenser**
I drilled a hole through the lid and mouth of a commercial snuff tin, just below the lock ring. To dispense snuff, line up the holes and dab out onto a thumbnail. Simply twist the lid to close the hole.

RattlerViper (2021): Nasal Snuff—4 Different Versions

Gletscherprise (original recipe from YouTube's Snus At Home, but I have made some alterations)
- 100 g tobacco flour
- 40 g distilled water
- 32 g mineral oil
- 8 g sea salt
- 2 g vegetable glycerin
- 6 g menthol
- 2 g camphor
- 12 g eucalyptus oil
- 7 g sodium carbonate

Anise Schmalzer
- 100 g tobacco flour
- 40 g distilled water
- 32 g mineral oil
- 6 g sea salt
- 2 g vegetable glycerin
- 2 **drams** LorAnn Anise flavoring
- 6 g sodium carbonate

I have found I can just alter the flavorings. Thus far I have tried buttered rum and peach as well (both LorAnn flavorings).

Clove dry snuff
- 50 g tobacco flour
- 5 g sea salt
- 3 g sodium carbonate
- 2 **drams** LorAnn Clove
- just enough distilled water to dissolve the sodium carbonate and sea salt

After it was all mixed, I spread it on a cookie sheet and baked it at 150°F to remove the water. I like this recipe quite a lot.

Cherry dry snuff

- 50 g tobacco flour
- 4 g sea salt
- 3 g sodium carbonate
- 1 **dram** LorAnn cherry
- 1 **dram** LorAnn Cinnamon Roll (Cherry by itself was not right, this was a huge improvement to me.)
- just enough distilled water to dissolve the sodium carbonate and sea salt

After it was all mixed I spread it on a cookie sheet and baked it at 150°F to remove the water.

I use mostly dark air-cured tobacco. I use a coffee grinder and run it through a very fine sieve to make sure there is no big stuff left.

Sodium carbonate: I utilized 7 g for 100 g of tobacco on my first batch, and went down to 6 g per 100 g. After further testing, I believe that I should always go with 3-4% (by weight) of sodium carbonate.

COMMENTS:
Tommy Tobaccoseed (2021)
I'm not the original poster, but I have made my own snuff in the past.

First, make sure your tobacco is as dry as possible before grinding, this is important for creating a fine flour.

I first used a blade type coffee grinder, which required shaking while it was running to keep the tobacco distributed. Later, I used a rather entry-level burr style coffee grinder that I found cheap at a thrift store. The burr grinder required sending the material through the machine several times to get it fine enough, most likely because it isn't the greatest piece of equipment. Of this I can't be certain, since I have no experience with a better machine. I then cobbled together a ball mill using a stainless steel vacuum bottle (thermos), some ½" ball bearings, and a drill running at low speed. This produced pretty good results, but it took a long time to do so.

There were trade-offs to each grinding method. I was only grinding rather small amounts at a time, around a couple ounces each batch.

Once the tobacco was ground, I sieved it for a more consistent particle size. I accomplished this by partially filling a mason jar with the flour, then placing a piece of pantyhose across the mouth of the jar, which is held in place by screwing the jar's ring over it. I was careful not to stretch the nylon material, as this will enlarge the holes in the nylon, and allow larger particles than desired through. The jar was then inverted, and shaken to move the material through the nylon mesh. This ended up being far too laborious, so I used an old barber's massager (which has a vibratory motor inside), held against the bottom of the inverted jar. That sped up the process exponentially. I also tried a palm sander, which worked okay. But the massager was better.

This process was messy and time consuming, and it made my hands numb from the vibration. But it produced some nice tobacco flour. There were, however, some fuzzy pieces present in the final product from the pantyhose, which I didn't care for. I would recommend purchasing some micron screen material to use instead. There are metal screens with a steel ring around them available for assorted purposes, or PVC ringed screens used for filtering plankton for research purposes, and they can be found easily on eBay. These can even be stacked to sort different particle sizes, as well.

Krausen89 (2021): Toast Nasal Snuff

- 3½ g Virginia flue-cured
- ½ tsp water
- 0.1 g sodium carbonate
- 0.2 g kosher salt

Toast leaves (no stem) at 200°F for 10 minutes, flip and toast other side for 10 minutes, then grind. Dissolve the sodium carbonate and salt in the water. Empty into a bowl with the tobacco and mix well. Spread onto parchment paper and toast at 200°F for another 10 minutes, or until crispy again. Pulverize in coffee grinder until super fine.

---

eebenz (2021): Toasted *Rustica* Nasal Snuff

I made this from *N. rustica* (Durman 904). I picked three yellow leaves from plants and dried them in oven. As I don't have a scale, I roughly measured the amount of powder with a scale made from coins and two rulers. Then I added ¾ tsp of this solution to it.

- 1 tsp salt
- 1¼ tsp sodium carbonate
- 74 ml water (~5 tbsp)

So the carbonate amount in final product should be something like 6.5%. Of course there is a lot of measurement error, so the amount can be even higher. But *rustica* is so acidic that it compensates.

After baking, grinding (by hand) and running it through tea strainer, it smells and tastes nice, and also hits pretty good.

Other Preparations

Making Sodium Carbonate (washing soda) from Baking Soda:

Heat baking soda (sodium bicarbonate) on a sheet pan in the oven at 200°F for 1 hour. Cool, then store in an air-tight container. *[Moisture will convert the sodium carbonate back into sodium bicarbonate.]*

_____

CobGuy (2017): North African Makla (oral)

The figures below are for 100 g of final product.
* tobacco is 35% chopped *N. rustica* and 65% "other"
* tobacco 37.7 g
* water 49 g
* calcium hydroxide 4.5 g
* calcium carbonate 5.5 g
* Magnesium carbonate hydroxide 0.5 g
* activated carbon 0.6 g
* disodium hydrogen phosphate 0.4 g
* edible oil 1.9 g

If I were to replicate this, I'd just dial back the alkali, and add some flavor.

COMMENTS:
Hasse SWE (2017): normally pH level in Swedish "snus" is around 8-8.5, but Makla has a pH range of 10.5 -10.9.

_____

CORESTA Smokeless Tobacco Reference Product

STRP 1S1 - Loose-leaf –Chewing Tobacco

Manufactured in January 1986

STRP 1S1 is an American-style loose-leaf smokeless tobacco product that was produced without added flavorings, except for those required to produce a product that is characteristic of the style. The reference product is packaged in foil pouches that contain 85g of product.

The target product composition supplied by the manufacturer is given below:

Component	% (wwb)
Wisconsin Air-cured tobacco	17.40
Pennsylvania Air-cured tobacco	15.47
Crushed Burley Tobacco Stems	5.80
Sodium chloride	1.60
Sodium propionate	0.28
Glycerin	3.75
Sucrose	23.01
Dextrose	1.70
Maltose	1.30
Corn syrup solids	6.21
Water	23.48
Total	**100**

wwb: wet weight basis

The following parameters were determined at the time of manufacture:

Parameter	Value
Moisture content	23.2 %
pH	6.4
Nicotine content	0.76 % (wwb)

wwb: wet weight basis

CORESTA Smokeless Tobacco Reference Product

STRP 2S1 - Loose-leaf –Chewing Tobacco

Manufactured in August 1998

STRP 2S1 is an American-style loose-leaf smokeless tobacco product that was produced
without added flavorings, except for those required to produce a product that is characteristic of
the style. The reference product is packaged in foil pouches that contain 85g of product.

The target product composition supplied by the manufacturer is given below:

Component	% (wwb)
Wisconsin Air-cured tobacco	17.40
Pennsylvania Air-cured tobacco	15.47
Crushed Burley Tobacco Stems	5.80
Sodium chloride	1.60
Sodium propionate	0.28
Glycerin	3.75
Sucrose	23.01
Dextrose	1.70
Maltose	1.30
Corn syrup solids	6.21
Water	23.48
Total	**100**

wwb: wet weight basis

The following parameters were determined at the time of manufacture:

Parameter	Value
Moisture content	21.99 %
pH	5.8
Nicotine content	0.84 % (wwb)

wwb: wet weight basis

CORESTA Smokeless Tobacco Reference Product
CRP4 - Loose-leaf

Manufactured in 2009

CRP4 is an American-style loose-leaf smokeless tobacco product that was produced without added flavorings, except for those required to produce a product that is characteristic of the style. The reference product is packaged in foil pouches that contain 85g of product.

The target product composition supplied by the manufacturer is given below:

Component	% (wwb)
Air-cured tobacco	30.7
Air-cured stem	5.4
Sodium chloride	1.9
Sodium propionate	0.2
Glycerin	3.2
Sucrose	25.9
Dextrose	2.0
Maltose	1.5
Corn syrup solids	7.2
Water	22.0
Total	**100**

wwb: wet weight basis

The following parameters were determined at the time of manufacture:

Parameter	Value
Moisture content	22 %
pH	6.0
Nicotine content	1.2 % (wwb)

wwb: wet weight basis

CORESTA Smokeless Tobacco Reference Product

CRP4.1- Chopped Loose-leaf

Manufactured in January 2016

CRP4.1 is a chopped American-style loose-leaf smokeless tobacco product that was produced without added flavorings, except for those required to produce a product that is characteristic of the style. The reference product is packaged in plastic cans that contain 28g of product.

The target product composition supplied by the manufacturer is given below:

Component	% (wwb)
Air-cured tobacco	32.4
Air-cured stem	5.8
Sodium chloride	1.8
Sodium propionate	0.3
Glycerin	6.8
Sucrose	10.9
Dextrose	3.5
Maltose	1.6
Corn syrup solids	13.9
Water	23.0
Total	**100**

wwb: wet weight basis

The following parameters were determined at the time of manufacture:

Parameter	Value
Moisture content	23 %
pH	6.2
Nicotine content	0.9 % (wwb)

wwb: wet weight basis

CORESTA Smokeless Tobacco Reference Product
CRP2 - Moist Snuff

Manufactured in 2009

CRP2 is an American-style loose moist snuff smokeless tobacco product that was produced without added flavorings, except for those required to produce a product that is characteristic of the style. The reference product is packaged in plastic cans that contain 34 grams of product.

The target product composition supplied by the manufacturer is given below:

Component	% (wwb)
Dark-fired tobacco	26.3
Air-cured tobacco	8.0
Burley Stem	3.8
Sodium carbonate	0.3
Sodium chloride	7.2
Water	54.4
Total	**100**

wwb: wet weight basis

The following parameters were determined at the time of manufacture:

Parameter	Value
Moisture content	54.6 %
pH	7.7
Nicotine content	1.2 % (wwb)

wwb: wet weight basis

CORESTA Smokeless Tobacco Reference Product
CRP2.1- Moist Snuff

Manufactured in April 2016

CRP2.1 is an American-style loose moist snuff smokeless tobacco product that was produced without added flavorings, except for those required to produce a product that is characteristic of the style. The reference product is packaged in plastic cans that contain 34 grams of product.

The target product composition supplied by the manufacturer is given below:

Component	% (wwb)
Dark-fired tobacco	26.6
Air-cured tobacco	8.1
Burley Stem	3.8
Sodium carbonate	0.5
Sodium chloride	8.0
Water	53.0
Total	**100**

wwb: wet weight basis

The following parameters were determined at the time of manufacture:

Parameter	Value
Moisture content	53 %
pH	7.7
Nicotine content	1.2 % (wwb)

wwb: wet weight basis

CORESTA Smokeless Tobacco Reference Product
CRP1 - Swedish Snus

Manufactured in 2009

CRP1 is a Swedish-style snus smokeless tobacco product that was produced without added flavorings, except for those required to produce a product that is characteristic of the style. The reference product is packaged in plastic cans that contain twenty four 1g pouches.

The target product composition supplied by the manufacturer is given below:

Component	% (wwb)
Dark air-cured lamina	25.5
Dark air-cured stem	20.8
Propylene glycol	3.0
Sodium carbonate	2.4
Sodium chloride	3.6
Water	44.7
Total	**100**

wwb: wet weight basis

The following parameters were determined at the time of manufacture:

Parameter	Value
Moisture content	52 %
pH	8.5
Nicotine content	0.8 % (wwb)

wwb: wet weight basis

CORESTA Smokeless Tobacco Reference Product

CRP1.1- Swedish Snus

Manufactured in January 2016

CRP1.1 is a Swedish-style snus smokeless tobacco product that was produced without added flavorings, except for those required to produce a product that is characteristic of the style. The reference product is packaged in plastic cans that contain twenty four 1g pouches.

The target product composition supplied by the manufacturer is given below:

Component	% (wwb)
Air-cured tobacco	8.4
Air-cured stem	0.2
Sun-cured tobacco	5.4
Sun-cured stem	9.7
Flue-cured stem	12.8
Propylene glycol	2.2
Sodium carbonate	1.8
Sodium chloride	4.0
Water	51.4
Pouch paper	4.1
Total	**100**

wwb: wet weight basis

The following parameters were determined at the time of manufacture:

Parameter	Value
Moisture content	53.7 %
pH	8.4
Nicotine content	0.8 % (wwb)

wwb: wet weight basis

CORESTA Smokeless Tobacco Reference Product
CRP3 - Dry Snuff

Manufactured in 2009

CRP3 is an American-style loose dry snuff smokeless tobacco product that was produced without added flavorings, except for those required to produce a product that is characteristic of the style. The reference product is packaged in plastic cans that contain 34 g of product.

The target product composition supplied by the manufacturer is given below:

Component	% (wwb)
Dark-fired tobacco	16.4
Air cured tobacco	51.2
Burley Stem	21.4
Sodium carbonate	2.0
Sodium chloride	1.0
Water	8.0
Total	**100**

wwb: wet weight basis

The following parameters were determined at the time of manufacture:

Parameter	Value
Moisture content	8.0%
pH	6.9
Nicotine content	1.9% (wwb)

wwb: wet weight basis

CORESTA Smokeless Tobacco Reference Product

CRP3.1- Dry Snuff

Manufactured in April 2016

CRP3.1 is an American-style loose dry snuff smokeless tobacco product that was produced without added flavorings, except for those required to produce a product that is characteristic of the style. The reference product is packaged in plastic cans that contain 34 g of product.

The target product composition supplied by the manufacturer is given below:

Component	% (wwb)
Dark-fired tobacco	54.8
Burley Stem	33.6
Sodium carbonate	1.1
Sodium chloride	1.1
Ammonium carbonate	1.4
Water	8.0
Total	**100**

wwb: wet weight basis

The following parameters were determined at the time of manufacture:

Parameter	Value
Moisture content	8.1%
pH	7.1
Nicotine content	1.7% (wwb)

wwb: wet weight basis

CORESTA Smokeless Tobacco Reference Product
STRP 1S2- Dry Snuff

Manufactured in February 1986

STRP 1S2 is an American-style loose dry snuff smokeless tobacco product that was produced without added flavorings, except for those required to produce a product that is characteristic of the style. The reference product is packaged in metal cans that contain 130 g of product.

The target product composition supplied by the manufacturer is given below:

Component	% (wwb)
Dark-fired tobacco	22.75
Fire Cured Virginia Tobacco	19.66
Air Cured Tobacco Stem	33.03
Flue Cured Tobacco Stem	15.20
Sodium Chloride**	0.36
Water	9.00
Total	**100**

wwb: wet weight basis

** Added salt does not include the natural salts found in tobacco.

The following parameters were determined at the time of manufacture:

Parameter	Value
Moisture content	11.75
pH	6.3
Nicotine content	1.32% (wwb)

wwb: wet weight basis

More detailed information on the chemical composition of this product may be found by clicking on the "Publications" link on the right of the home page.

All ingredients are listed in descending order by weight.

Bruton Dry Snuff
Bruton Scotch Snuff
tobacco
water
ammonium carbonate
sodium chloride (salt)
sodium carbonate
preservatives

Carhart Dry Snuff
C.C. Carhart's Choice
tobacco
water
natural and artificial flavors
ammonium carbonate
sodium chloride (salt)
sodium carbonate
sodium saccharin
preservatives
maltodextrin
silicon dioxide

Copenhagen
Copenhagen Snuff Fine Cut
water
tobacco
sodium chloride (salt)
natural and artificial flavors
ethyl alcohol
sodium carbonate
ammonium carbonate
preservatives

Copenhagen Extra Long Cut Natural
water
tobacco
sodium chloride (salt)
binders
natural and artificial flavors
ethyl alcohol
sodium carbonate
ammonium carbonate
preservatives

Copenhagen Long Cut
water
tobacco
sodium chloride (salt)
binders
natural and artificial flavors
ammonium chloride
ethyl alcohol
ammonium carbonate
sodium carbonate
preservatives

Copenhagen Neat Cut Natural
water
tobacco
sodium chloride (salt)
cotton fabric
binders
natural and artificial flavors
ethyl alcohol
sodium carbonate
ammonium carbonate
preservatives

Copenhagen Long Cut Black
water
tobacco
sodium chloride (salt)
natural and artificial flavors
binders
ammonium carbonate
ethyl alcohol
ammonium chloride
sodium carbonate
glycerol
sodium saccharin
preservatives

Copenhagen Long Cut Mint
water
tobacco
sodium chloride (salt)
natural and artificial flavors
binders
ammonium carbonate
sodium carbonate
ethyl alcohol
sodium saccharin
sucralose
preservatives

Copenhagen Neat Cut Mint
water
tobacco
sodium chloride (salt)
natural and artificial flavors
cotton fabric
binders
sodium carbonate
ammonium carbonate
sodium saccharin
ethyl alcohol
sucralose
preservatives

Copenhagen Neat Cut Wintergreen
water
tobacco
sodium chloride
natural and artificial flavors
cotton fabric
binders
sodium carbonate
ammonium carbonate
sucralose
sodium saccharin
preservatives
ethyl alcohol

Copenhagen Long Cut Southern Blend
water
tobacco
sodium chloride (salt)
binders
natural and artificial flavors
ammonium chloride
ammonium carbonate
ethyl alcohol
sodium carbonate
sodium saccharin
propylene glycol
preservatives
sucralose

Copenhagen Fine Cut Wintergreen
water
tobacco
sodium Chloride (salt)
natural and artificial flavors
binders
sodium carbonate
ammonium carbonate
ethyl alcohol
sodium saccharin
sucralose
preservatives

Copenhagen Long Cut Straight
water
tobacco
sodium chloride (salt)
natural and artificial flavors
binders
sodium carbonate
ammonium carbonate
ethyl alcohol
sodium saccharin
preservatives

Copenhagen Extra Fine Cut
Natural
water
tobacco
sodium chloride (salt)
natural and artificial flavors
ethyl alcohol
sodium carbonate
ammonium carbonate
preservatives

Copenhagen Long Cut Wintergreen
water
tobacco
natural and artificial flavors
sodium chloride (salt)
binders
ammonium carbonate
sodium carbonate
sodium saccharin
sucralose
preservatives
ethyl alcohol

DeVoe Dry Snuff
DeVoe Sweet Scotch Snuff
tobacco
water
natural and artificial flavors
ammonium carbonate
sodium chloride (salt)
sodium carbonate
sodium saccharin
preservatives
maltodextrin
silicon dioxide

Red Seal Dry Snuff
tobacco
water
natural and artificial flavors
ammonium carbonate
sodium chloride (salt)
sodium carbonate
sodium saccharin
preservatives

Red Seal
Red Seal Fine Cut Natural
water
tobacco
sodium chloride (salt)
natural and artificial flavors
ethyl alcohol
sodium carbonate
ammonium carbonate
preservatives

Red Seal Long Cut Natural
water
tobacco
sodium chloride (salt)
natural and artificial flavors
ammonium chloride
ethyl alcohol
ammonium carbonate
sodium carbonate
preservatives

**Red Seal Fine Cut
Wintergreen**
water
tobacco
sodium chloride (salt)
natural and artificial flavors
ethyl alcohol
sodium carbonate
ammonium carbonate
sodium saccharin
preservatives

Red Seal Long Cut Straight
water
tobacco
sodium chloride (salt)
natural and artificial flavors
sodium citrate
ammonium carbonate
ammonium chloride
sodium carbonate
sodium carboxymethylcellulose
sodium saccharin
preservatives
ethyl alcohol

Red Seal Long Cut Mint
water
tobacco
sodium chloride (salt)
natural and artificial flavors
sodium citrate
ammonium carbonate
ammonium chloride
sodium carbonate
sodium carboxymethylcellulose
sodium saccharin
preservatives
ethyl alcohol

**Red Seal Long Cut
Wintergreen**
water
tobacco
sodium chloride (salt)
natural and artificial flavors
Ethyl Alcohol
sodium carbonate
ammonium carbonate
sodium saccharin
preservatives

**Rooster Dry Snuff
Rooster Snuff**
tobacco
water
ammonium carbonate
sodium chloride (salt)
sodium carbonate
preservatives

**Skoal
Skoal Original Fine Cut**
Wintergreen
water
tobacco
sodium chloride (salt)
natural and artificial flavors
ethyl alcohol
sodium carbonate
ammonium carbonate
sodium saccharin
preservatives

Skoal Cool Green Long Cut
water
tobacco
sodium chloride (salt)
natural and artificial flavors
binders
sodium carbonate
ammonium carbonate
sodium saccharin
ethyl alcohol
preservatives

Skoal Long Cut Apple Tobacco Blend

water
tobacco
sodium chloride (salt)
natural and artificial flavors
sodium citrate
ethyl alcohol
ammonium chloride
ammonium carbonate
propylene glycol
sodium carbonate
sodium saccharin
preservatives

Skoal X-tra Long Cut Crisp Blend

water
tobacco
sodium chloride (salt)
natural and artificial flavors
binders
ethyl alcohol
propylene glycol
sodium carbonate
ammonium carbonate
sodium saccharin
preservatives

Skoal Long Cut Berry Tobacco Blend

water
tobacco
sodium chloride (salt)
natural and artificial flavors
sodium carbonate
ammonium carbonate
ethyl alcohol
propylene glycol
sodium saccharin
preservatives

Skoal X-tra Long Cut Rich Blend

water
tobacco
sodium chloride (salt)
natural and artificial flavors
binders
sodium carbonate
ethyl alcohol
ammonium carbonate
propylene glycol
sodium citrate
sodium saccharin
preservatives

Skoal Long Cut Cherry Tobacco Blend

water
tobacco
sodium chloride (salt)
natural and artificial flavors
sodium carbonate
ammonium carbonate
propylene glycol
ethyl alcohol
sodium saccharin
preservatives
sodium bicarbonate

Skoal X-tra Long Cut Wintergreen Blend

water
tobacco
sodium chloride (salt)
natural and artificial flavors
binders
sodium carbonate
ammonium carbonate
ethyl alcohol
sodium saccharin
preservatives

Skoal Long Cut Citrus Tobacco Blend

water
tobacco
sodium chloride (salt)
natural and artificial flavors
sodium citrate
ammonium chloride
ammonium carbonate
sodium carbonate
propylene glycol
ethyl alcohol
sucralose
preservatives

Skoal X-tra Long Cut Mint Blend

water
tobacco
sodium chloride (salt)
natural and artificial flavors
binders
sodium carbonate
ammonium carbonate
sodium saccharin
ethyl alcohol
preservatives

Skoal Long Cut Peach Tobacco Blend
water
tobacco
sodium chloride (salt)
natural and artificial flavors
propylene glycol
sodium citrate
ethyl alcohol
ammonium chloride
ammonium carbonate
sodium carbonate
sucralose
preservatives

Skoal Long Cut Mint
water
tobacco
sodium chloride (salt)
natural and artificial flavors
binders
sodium carbonate
ammonium carbonate
sodium saccharin
ethyl alcohol
preservatives

Skoal Long Cut Classic
water
tobacco
sodium chloride (salt)
natural and artificial flavors
ethyl alcohol
sodium carbonate
ammonium carbonate
preservatives
sodium saccharin

Skoal Long Cut Wintergreen
water
tobacco
sodium chloride (salt)
natural and artificial flavors
binders
sodium carbonate
ammonium carbonate
ethyl alcohol
sodium saccharin
preservatives

Skoal Long Cut Spearmint
water
tobacco
sodium chloride (salt)
natural and artificial flavors
sodium carbonate
ammonium carbonate
ethyl alcohol
sodium saccharin
preservatives

Skoal Neat Cut Wintergreen
water
tobacco
sodium chloride (salt)
natural and artificial flavors
cotton fabric
binders
sodium carbonate
ammonium carbonate
ethyl alcohol
sodium saccharin
sucralose
preservatives

Skoal Long Cut Straight
water
tobacco
sodium chloride (salt)
natural and artificial flavors
binders
sodium carbonate
ammonium carbonate
sodium saccharin
ethyl alcohol
preservatives

Skoal Read Cut Rich Blend
water
tobacco
sodium chloride (salt)
natural and artificial flavors
binders
ethyl alcohol
propylene glycol
sodium carbonate
ammonium carbonate
sodium saccharin
sucralose
preservatives

Skoal Snus
Skoal Snus Mint
tobacco
water
fiber
propylene glycol
pouch materials
natural and artificial flavors
sodium chloride (salt)
potassium carbonate
binder
sucralose

Skoal Snus Smooth Mint
tobacco
water
fiber
pouch materials
propylene glycol
natural and artificial flavors
sodium chloride (salt)
potassium carbonate
binder
sucralose

Standard Dry Snuff
Standard "S" Scotch Snuff
tobacco
water
ammonium carbonate
sodium chloride (salt)
sodium carbonate
preservatives

WB
WB Cut
tobacco
water
sodium chloride (salt)
natural and artificial flavors
ethyl alcohol
sodium carbonate
preservatives
propylene glycol

see page 73, for ingredients of **Swedish Match** *products*
Red Man
Red Man Golden Blend
Red Man Silver Blend
Red Man Select
Granger Select
Work Horse
Brown Mule's Plug
Natural Leaf Plug
Red Man Plug
Tinsley Plug

Made in the USA
Middletown, DE
18 October 2023